Family at Large

An Entertaining Peek into the Life of a Large Family

Joanne Schreuders

FAMILY AT LARGE
Copyright © 2024 by Joanne Schreuders

All rights reserved. Neither this publication nor any part of this publication may be reproduced or transmitted in any form or by any means, electronic or mechanical, including photocopying, recording or any information storage and retrieval system, without permission in writing from the author.

Scripture quotations are taken from THE HOLY BIBLE, NEW INTERNATIONAL VERSION®, NIV® Copyright © 1973, 1978, 1984, 2011 by Biblica, Inc.® Used by permission. All rights reserved worldwide.

Printed in Canada

ISBN: 978-1-4866-2550-5
eBook ISBN: 978-1-4866-2551-2

Word Alive Press
119 De Baets Street Winnipeg, MB R2J 3R9
www.wordalivepress.ca

WORD ALIVE
—PRESS—

MIX
Paper from
responsible sources
FSC® C103567

Cataloguing in Publication information can be obtained from Library and Archives Canada.

To my Super God! Thanks for always being there for me, even on those days when, to me, you felt so far away.

Thanks to my loving and supportive husband (and awesome father to our ten kids), who has kept his promise to me. Life with you is exciting and never dull!

Thanks to Derek, Desiree, Nicolas, Nathan, Victoria, Christina, Elly, Melissa, Calvin, and Joshua for helping Dad keep life in our house ... interesting.

Thanks for all you have taught me.

I thank God every day for placing each of you in my life. I love you all dearly!

Contents

One:	It All Started When	1
Two:	Are You Going to Have More?	9
Three:	Old Mac Schreuders' Farm	12
Four:	The One That Got Left Behind	17
Five:	How Do You House a Large Family?	20
Six:	Answered Prayer	25
Seven:	Chocolate Chip Cookies	48
Eight:	Surprise Vacation	51
Nine:	Mom to the Rescue!	56
Ten:	Finding God	60
Eleven:	Always Expect the Unexpected	65
Twelve:	Lifestyle	70
Thirteen:	What about Me?	75
Fourteen:	Camping	79
Fifteen:	Date Night	84
Sixteen:	Unpredictable Bunnies	88
Seventeen:	Inconvenience	94
Eighteen:	A Large Family Sort of Day	97
Nineteen:	Things People Say!	100
Twenty:	Thoughts from My Parenting Experience By Jim Schreuders (Oct. 2012)	105
	Also by Joanne Schreuders	107

One
It All Started When

IT ALL BEGAN on that cold wintery day of Monday, December 12, 1988. I was eighteen and in my first year of college. While I was taking computer courses, Jim, at twenty-one, was working the family farm. We lived two hours away from each other, so it took work to find time to spend together. Finding ways to communicate over a long distance wasn't easy, as there was no texting, skype, MSN, or emailing. So we had to write letters or talk on the phone, the latter of which would cost money as soon as the minutes started to tick away. We would usually take turns driving out on weekends to one or the other's houses. But we didn't mind; we were in *love*.

Having dated for a year, I wanted to spend the day together. I was at Jim's house for the weekend while trying to study for an exam I had to write later that day. Jim kept asking me when I was leaving.

"Wouldn't it be better to study at school?" he asked.

My heart was broken. It was our first anniversary, but somehow this day didn't seem special to him. It seemed as though he didn't want to spend the day with me. Instead, he kept pushing me away. He told me he would see me that evening when he would take my parents and me out for dinner. Why would he bother driving two hours to go out for dinner and then drive the two hours home again? Confused, I thought, *I'm right here, and you don't seem to want to spend time with me.* In a helpless huff, I gathered my things and prepared to leave for school, which was a little more than an hour away on the route home. I mumbled goodbye and told him I'd see him that evening. Then, feeling dejected, I made my way to school to write the exam.

Well, unfortunately, the exam did not go well. I was having a hard time concentrating on the test. *Why is he pushing me away? I love him! Is he going to tell me this is the end of our relationship?* The words on the exam paper started to swim. I told myself, *Think about that later. Think about the exam now ... write! God help me through this. I know I was giving up liking guys and was going to concentrate on school, but he just sauntered into my life with that amazing, sweet smile ... exam ... write.*

"Where's Jim?" my dad asked later that day as he entered the kitchen, all dressed in his Sunday best. Mom, dressed in her best, looked over at me where I sat fidgeting at the table. I shrugged my shoulders as my stomach turned with worry. I wondered if he was even going to come. Then my heart did one of its flip-flops as I heard him striding up the sidewalk. I jumped up immediately.

"He's here!" I announced as I rushed to meet him at the back door. Thankfully, I didn't have to answer any more questions. He entered with a tight clean t-shirt, his perfectly-fitting jeans, and carrying his Sunday suit.

"Just got to change; be just a minute. I'll meet you in the Jimmy," he announced as my parents and I parted like the Red Sea to let him pass. My dad shook his head with disappointment as my mom asked questions I didn't know how to answer.

"Jim made all the plans. You'll have to ask him," I told them as we made our way outside to Jim's Jimmy.

Later, as we all sat stiffly in a fancy restaurant, The Castle Del Tora, we celebrated my mom and dad's twentieth anniversary and

It All Started When

our first year together. There were red velvet drapes, candlelight, and a menu full of beautiful fancy words I didn't understand. I think we all felt like we didn't belong there. I peeked over at Jim. He seemed to be fidgety. I reached for his hand under the table and squeezed it. He glanced up at me. I smiled, trying to put him at ease, only to receive a nervous smile back. My heart sank some more, wondering what was going through his head. My parents were talking now and seemed to be enjoying the delightful meal, not really noticing the tension between Jim and me. At one point in the dinner, Jim asked to be excused to go to the "powder room." When he returned, he said, more confidently, that he had a surprise for us after dinner.

"What is it?" I asked, noticing Jim relax a little more. Then I looked over to see a worried look in my dad's eyes.

"It won't be a surprise if I tell you," Jim grinned.

While he left to pay the bill, my dad leaned over to me with a twinkle in his eye and said, "If he embarrasses me in the slightest little bit, it will be *your* fault."

Shocked, I said, "Why would it be my fault? I don't know what he's up to!"

I wondered what had come over Jim as he came around the corner, ready to burst at the seams, asking if we were ready to go. Mom and I politely asked if we could first make a quick stop at the bathroom.

As we left the bathroom, we noticed the guys impatiently standing in the hall by the exit door. Jim was like a giddy schoolboy, ready to explode with anticipation, as if he was about to observe the teacher opening the desk drawer with the frog in it.

"Are you ready for your surprise?" he asked with great confidence.

"I guess," I answered. Jim opened the large wooden doors of the restaurant, letting Dad quickly guide Mom out and toward the Jimmy. A sleek, black stretch limo stood directly in front of us. The well-dressed limo driver smiled politely while he held the rear door open.

Shocked, I said, "You're kidding, right?"

Laughing, he said no, and we called my parents back.

"This is for us," I said as they turned back to the limo.

Astonished, Dad said, "You're kidding, right?"

Is there an echo? I wondered as my parents joined us in the limo.

Jim and Dad had fun playing with all the buttons, as it was the first time for all of us to ride in a limo. Mom and I sat back and enjoyed the boys' antics, looking forward to the exciting destination Jim had just told us about—Niagara Falls, about a fifteen-minute drive away. We looked forward to the awesome light display that was put on there this time of year.

At the falls, Jim picked up the car phone and telephoned the driver, asking him to pull over so we could get out for a walk. I looked down at my mini-skirt, and my teeth immediately began chattering. But Jim lovingly smiled at me, and my heart warmed as I prepared myself for the cold walk in the wet, misty night air. Mom and Dad went to the left, down from the falls. Jim and I headed right toward the thunder. I was used to going there with crowds of people, people everywhere. This night we were the only ones there. It was almost still, an eerie night, yet maybe even romantic ... okay, definitely romantic. The thunder of the falls echoed in my ears as the cold mist surrounded us. Finally, we stopped where the water crests over the falls. I cuddled up to Jim, craving the warmth he gave as he pulled me in closer. He kissed me tenderly. As I slowly pulled back, my hands went out to his chest.

I loudly whispered over the thunder, "I'm cold. Can we go back now?"

But wait, what does he have in his jacket pocket?

Lovingly, he looked down at me and said, "Yes, but I have to ask you a question." He took a small step back, reached into his jacket pocket, and smoothly pulled out a small, velvety box. My mind whirled, my heart stopped, my eyes leaked, and my jaw dropped. "Will you marry me?" The box opened, and a ring swam before my eyes. My hands shook as they covered my mouth.

"You're kidding, right?" I cried. He smiled from ear to ear; his laughter rang like music in my ears.

I jumped into his arms and held him tight as he said, "I take that as a yes?"

I laughed as I said, "*Yes!*" and swiped away the tears while Jim placed the ring on my finger. I looked down at the sparkling ring, still unable to see it fully through my tears.

Jim said, "You have to hide it because I haven't asked your dad yet!"

What? He hadn't asked my dad yet? Oh great, how will that go? I always knew that my dad wanted to be asked for his permission first. So what would he say now? Swiping at the last tears and hiding my ring hand in Jim's hand, we returned to the limo, smiling. Mom and Dad had also just made it back, so we all hopped back into the warm vehicle. Dad spied the bottle of wine and suggested we open it.

Jim respectfully said, "First, I have a question to ask you. I've asked Joanne to marry me, and I'd like your permission to do so." New tears rolled down my cheeks as Dad's jaw just dropped.

Mom started talking rapidly. "This is so neat! This is so neat! Oh, this is so neat!" Then she noticed Jim looking at Dad. "Sorry, he asked you," she finished as she turned to look at Dad.

Dad, still sitting there in shock, slowly picked up his jaw. With his hitchhiker's thumb, he pointed to Mom and said, "What she said."

Jim's smile reappeared; he reached over to the bottle of wine and opened it. Mom started talking again. I showed off the ring, and I wondered if the tears would ever stop so that I could finally get a chance to see it myself.

Family at Large

Soon after, we were making our way back to the restaurant, where it was agreed that Dad and Mom would drive Jim's Jimmy back home. The limo driver informed us that he needed gas, so it would take a little longer to get home. More time together in the limo? That was okay with us! It would give Jim time to recap the day from his point of view. Apparently, he was trying to encourage me to go to school so that he could make phone calls to confirm everything. Unfortunately, he had to work on the farm before he could leave, and I would only be a distraction. As I looked at him now in the limo, I knew he was right. I gave him a sly smile and kissed him. He asked me if I had seen all the snow on his shoes when he came back from the "powder room." Apparently, he saw the limo pull into the parking lot outside the window. This was why he excused himself—to talk to the driver. At that time, he also put the wine and mood music into the limo, which he had carefully stashed in his Jimmy.

While holding my hand and turning the ring, he informed me that he had bought the ring nine months ago. He wanted to finish the payments before giving it to me. He smiled at me and said, "You were sleeping on it all that time." At my puzzled expression, he explained that when I was over at his house and he slept on the couch while I slept in his room, the ring was under the bed. We continued to talk a little about wedding dates, hopes, and dreams. He promised me that life with him would be exciting and never dull.

I grew up in a peaceful little town, at the end of the street surrounded by Beaver Creek. My grandma and grandpa lived beside us in the second-last house. My dad was the second of five boys, and I was the first girl in the family and the oldest grandchild. I treasured my relationship with my grandparents and was eager to share this night with them. Having easily made it home before us, Dad ran into Grandma and Grandpa's house, interrupting the evening news.

"Don't go to bed yet. We have a surprise!" Then he ran out again. Puzzled, my grandparents watched him as he ran off and sped home to wake up my brother and sister.

A short time later, Grandma and Grandpa heard another vehicle coming down the road.

"It's a limo. Someone must be lost. Are they stopping here? The driver is getting out. It's Jim and Joanne. What?"

Grandma and Grandpa came to meet us at the door with puzzled looks on their faces.

We smiled, and I blurted out, "Jim asked me to marry him!"

"You're kidding, right?" said Grandpa.

"Where have I heard that before?" Jim laughed.

We all hugged, shared tears, showed off the ring, and hugged again. They had happy tears. I was so fortunate that they could be part of that special day. They were so dear to me, and it meant so much that they approved of Jim too. As we said good night, I wondered if any of us would get any sleep that night.

At home, my sister, sixteen, and brother, twelve, were not too impressed with being awakened. My mom was rummaging in the basement, and she finally appeared with some boxes.

"I know that they aren't wrapped, but here is your engagement gift," she said as she set the boxes in front of Jim and me. I was shocked to see an eight-piece dinnerware set.

"Someone, please pinch me. This is not how I thought this day would go. What started as distressing became my own personal fairy tale!"

Joanne: "If God gives you a talent, shouldn't you use it?"

Jim: "I have not figured out my talent yet."

Teenage son: "Isn't it to be fruitful and multiply?"

Family at Large

You know you have a large family when ...

- *Your co-worker says, "If you were a superhero, you'd be called The Multiplier!"*
- *Your husband says, "Movies just aren't as exciting anymore. My life is more exciting."*
- *You feel you change the toilet paper roll every time you go to the bathroom.*
- *Your fridge is covered with more photos of your own kids than your friend's families.*
- *Someone accidentally taps the video call on your family messenger app and over five people suddenly join in. To cover up her error, she asks, "Doesn't anyone work around here?" and proceeds to hang up.*
- *You find a child sitting in their car, in the driveway, for peace and quiet.*

TWO
Are You Going to Have More?

ONE BEAUTIFUL JUNE day, I decided to be brave and take my six children to Stratford. This would be our first outing since Christina had been born only a few weeks earlier. With Christina in the snuggly, I pushed Nathan and Vicky in the double stroller. Nico and Desiree each obediently held a side of the double stroller. We leisurely walked the gentle upward slope from the library toward uptown. Derek, who was walking beside me, kept the conversation going. When we reached the stoplight, we had to turn left to cross the busy street. Ahead of us came two ladies who whispered loudly, "Three-four-five-six." Then came the question everyone asked: "Are they all yours?"

I thought I was up for this. Let's have some fun.

"Yes, they are. Now you have to ask the next question," came my reply.

"And what would that be?" the bold lady replied, slightly taken aback.

"Are there any twins?" I replied.

"Well, are there?" she asked with a smile.

"No," I said.

The light turned green, and I began herding my dutiful children across the bustling street. In all the commotion, I didn't realize that the fascinated lady was still closely watching me. If I had, it wouldn't have surprised me when she interrogated me with the next common question.

"Are you going to have any more?"

Thinking fast while continuing across the street, I said, "Well, I still haven't figured out how this is happening." Then, to my surprise, I was yanked to an abrupt halt in the middle of the intersection. Bustling cars surrounded me as my wide-eyed children wondered why we had stopped. I rapidly turned to see the shocked look on the astonished lady's flushed face. Still holding me in place by her sturdy hand, she firmly commanded, "Girl, you have to buy yourself a book!"

With that comment, she abruptly turned and continued to the other side of the street to join her friend. I stared after her, stunned that she thought I was serious. Suddenly I found myself standing in the middle of the street, with Derek urging me on. We continued on our way across the street and in the opposite direction of the bold ladies.

Later that night at dinner, I described the happenings of my day to Jim. Together we wondered if the well-intending lady really did think I was clueless. As we continued our meal, I thought about the rest of my day and started to laugh. Jim looked at me quizzically.

"I was just wondering if those ladies looked back and saw me go into the Christian bookstore!"

You never know what adventurous tales can be told when you venture out for a day with a large family!

———————————

You know you have a large family when ...

- *You don't pick up that sucker or chocolate bar at the checkout. On occasion, maybe a pack of gum because everyone can have a piece, but definitely not a sucker or chocolate bar.*
- *You purchase an industrial-size washing machine.*
- *You seriously consider buying industrial baking supplies, such as pans, mixers, ovens.*
- *You have more than one dinner time, and the table is full both times.*
- *Your dishwasher has been broken for more than five years, and you don't see the need to fix it because it's a way to make your teenagers spend time with you ... talking!*
- *The phone rings and you don't need to quickly finish in the bathroom because you know someone will answer it.*

Three
Old Mac Schreuders' Farm

"WOW! I CAN'T believe it. I'm at Old Mac Donald's Farm! Oh, sorry, I mean Old Mac Schreuders' farm!" announced our friends one day when they came for a visit.

At this time, we were renting a hobby farm—a great place for six kids to grow up. On our farm, we housed one dog, three cats, two bunnies, two cows with their three calves, two sheep, three pigs, meat chickens, a dozen laying chickens, and seven turkeys. It all started with the calves and cows, and then came the chickens, all to be raised for meat. Indoor pets weren't allowed due to my annoying allergies. I could often be heard using the excuse of too many kids, therefore no room for the dog, cats, and bunnies in the house.

The three smelly pigs were being raised for meat by our oldest son, Derek, to finance his trip to the International Camporee out west. We also enjoyed watching Nathan try to ride these bucking bronco pigs. Our oldest daughter, Desiree, had the laying chickens and sold the eggs for a little cash. The fuzzy sheep came "by accident." Jim was fixing a sheep farmer friend's baler one day, and since my husband wouldn't accept money for the repair, he offered Jim two of the triplet lambs. The white mother favoured one lamb and left the other brother and sister to fend for themselves.

After arriving home that day, Nico bounded excitedly into the house. "Guess what we got, Mom," he announced excitedly, followed closely by Derek.

"You weren't supposed to tell, Nico!" Derek reprimanded.

"Come see, Mom!" said Nico, not deterred, firmly taking me by the hand and leading me outside. There, bleating in the back of the covered pickup box, stood two fuzzy lambs, with my husband standing sheepishly nearby (no pun intended), saying, "I thought it might be fun!"

Next there were the quiet turkeys. Being our first try, we were going to raise them for Thanksgiving dinner. A friend, who also had a hobby farm, told us that they wouldn't be ready for Thanksgiving. So it was decided, then and there, to save them for Christmas dinner. Well, before long, the time came to bring them to the poultry butcher. Being the serious homeschooling family we were, every opportunity was taken to give our kids new experiences. So, of course, they all came with us.

First, Jim lined flattened cardboard boxes in the back of our GMC Astro van. He then backed the van up to the barn door. After placing an old feed sack over each turkey's head to calm them, he placed each of the seven plump turkeys in the back of the not-so-large trunk of our red van. The delighted boys ran the van doors, keeping the turkeys from wandering out while Jim went for the next feed-sacked turkey. After the fat turkeys were cleverly loaded, we corralled our half dozen kids into the now-tight van. Taking a deep breath, we headed cautiously to the well-known butcher about forty-five minutes away.

We heard some screaming from the back seat a little over halfway there. You know, the blood-curdling kind that makes the hair stand on the back of your neck? Whipping around, we could see all the kids leaning to the right. A curious turkey had escaped from the cramped feed bag and was now stretching its head around the back seat to investigate his new surroundings.

"It's out! It's out!" yelled Desiree before we heard another blood-curdling scream.

"We're almost there. It can't come into your seat. It's too fat to fit between the seat and the window," we reassured.

The kids looked at us with a look that showed they didn't believe us. Jim and I tried to keep our smiles and giggles to ourselves as we started coming up with newspaper headlines:

Seven Turkeys and Six Kids in Accident!
Driver Loses Control with Six Kids and Seven Turkeys!
Six Kids and Seven Turkeys Make Driver Lose Control

To the kids' relief, we arrived at the butcher in one piece. As the van came to a stop, the doors exploded open, and all the excited little humans tumbled out. Jim received instructions to back up to the large door, where an employee would help him unload.

After backing up to the door and gingerly opening the right rear door, Jim quickly grabbed the smallest turkey by the legs and hauled it out. With a shocked look, a gentleman of short stature stepped toward Jim to take the plump turkey from my husband's strained hands.

"Do you have anything smaller in there?" he asked, groaning under the weight. Jim returned his look with a surprise of his own.

"This *is* the small one," he replied.

As they struggled to hang up the turkeys in the processing plant, I couldn't help but smile as I overheard two farmers nearby say, "Wow! Look at the breast on that girl!"

The next day we returned to pick up our butchered turkeys. They each filled a cooler. The bags we took to put them in weren't big enough, so we had to borrow some garbage bags. On the way home, we stopped at the neighbour's house, who had agreed to lend us some freezer space. Two of the larger turkeys were dropped off in his freezer.

Old Mac Schreuders' Farm

At home, I placed the biggest turkey on the counter, preparing to cut it into smaller portions. Then the thought hit me: *Will this turkey even fit in the oven?* Oven? Yes. But in my large roasting pan? *Never!* How big was this turkey anyway? I grabbed the scale, stood on it, mentally recording the weight, and then grabbed the turkey. I did the math. I did the math ... *again.*

"*Jim!*" I hollered. "You better go get the other big turkey from the neighbour! They will never fit in the oven. This one is forty-seven pounds!"

Jim took a smaller turkey to the neighbour and traded it for the other big one. I weighed that one at fifty pounds! Each turkey took an hour to carve into meal-size portions of turkey roasts, chops, and legs. A leg fed our family for a meal! The meat was delightfully tender. We have never had anything like it before or since.

"I should have known they were ready when they didn't roost on the pen walls anymore," Jim voiced, shaking his head in surprise.

The following year, Jim called the butcher earlier to book our turkeys for processing.

"Hello. This is Jim Schreuders. I don't know if you remember me from last year," he said into the phone.

"Yes, sir, we definitely remember *you*!"

I guess our super-sized turkeys had become a bit of a legend! And there would always be a special place for Old Mac Schreuders' Farm in our family's "remember when" memories!

Family at Large

You know you have a large family when ...

- *You tell the inquisitive hairdresser you have ten children, to which she responds, "How many are his and hers?" To which I have to respond, "They are all ours!" I'm sure we both thought, <u>What is the world coming to?</u>*
- *A guest comes out of your bathroom laughing, "I have never seen so many toothbrushes in one cup before!"*
- *You seriously discuss buying a tiny place for a getaway from the kids.*
- *Younger children don't fear talking to big teenage boys who aren't related to them.*
- *There are many siblings to borrow stuff from. Better yet, when they can't remember who borrowed it, you get to keep it.*

Four
The One That Got Left Behind

"HELLO, MOM," I said abruptly into the phone. "We have officially become a large family today."

Mom was momentarily silent, so I knew she wasn't following my train of thought.

"We left a child behind at church!" I clarified.

Christina, at the age of three, was always hungry. Every Sunday, she would inform us that we were starving her once again on the way home from church. Well, on this particular sunny Sunday morning, the back of the van seemed blissfully quiet. After about five minutes, I turned around in the passenger seat of Big Blue (the name our kids gave to our large, twelve-passenger van) to check on our seven quiet children.

One – two – three – four – five – six. No. One – two – three boys. The boys were all here. One – two – three. *We're missing a girl*, I said to myself.

Desiree.

Vicky.

Baby Elizabeth

"Christina!" I shouted.

"Desiree, is Christina in the back seat with you?"

Glancing briefly from her book to her right, she nonchalantly yelled, *"Nope!"*

"Stop! Turn around! We're missing Christina!" I excitedly told Jim in a panic. "We must have left her at church!"

The poor little girl was only three. *She must be scared. How could I let this happen?* Sitting straighter in my seat, I tried to keep quiet and silently prayed: *Lord, please be with my little girl and keep her safe, safer than I have today.*

We were finally able to turn around and headed back toward the church. We passed dear friends of ours going the other way. We were a little confused to see them waving frantically at us. We concluded that they were telling us Christina was at the church, so we carried on.

In what felt like an eternity, we arrived at the nearly-empty church parking lot, only to see two cars left. I felt panic rise within me. Tears were on the verge of spilling as I thought of my little girl, frightened and possibly in tears, alone in the cold, dark church basement. The janitor sauntered up to us as we drove into the parking lot and told us that the friends we had just passed had taken her home. Well, that explained their frantic waving.

Turning around, we headed for home ... *again*. I felt relieved now, knowing she was safe with someone we knew. Then to our surprise, we passed the waving friends again. With a big sigh and a smile starting to pull at the corners of my mouth, I thought, *This could go on forever.*

I guess Jim was thinking the same thing, for he pulled the van over to the side of the road. Our friends turned around and drove up behind us. Frantically I jumped out, expecting to see my little girl in tears. Instead, with some encouragement, she got out of our friends' van, looking confused. Not at all what I expected. She was looking forward to visiting with her friends for the day, just as her older siblings regularly did.

The One That Got Left Behind

On the way home, we started to relax as we listened to her side of this interesting story. This was when we realized that I had thought Jim had put her in the van, and he'd thought I had. Then we had "the talk." You know—the talk about coming when you're told to, *right away*! After a big sigh, I sat back in my seat and tried to relax a little more. Then, with a smile, Jim leaned over and said, "I'm glad it's Mother's Day today and not Father's Day!"

Isn't Mother's Day a day when we celebrate the *real* moms who make mistakes?

You know you have a large family when ...
- *You look at a new van and the main question you ask each other is, "What are the laws about seat belts?"*
    a) Must every person have seat belts, or
    b) All seat belts must be in use?
- *Sweeping the floor means taking a broom to the outside edges of the room where all the dirt and dust bunnies have landed because the breeze of people's traffic pushed it there.*
- *It's a miracle if you can wash the floors without someone walking on them before they're dry or before you're finished washing them!*
- *When a spotless house is but a dream, and the feeling of a clean floor is short-lived.*

Five
How Do You House a Large Family?

AT THE BEGINNING of 1995, we moved into our new-to-us rental home. It was a quaint, old, one-and-a-half-storey stone house on a one-hundred-acre piece of property with a small bank barn outback, known to you as Old Mac Schreuders' Farm. It was perfect for our family of four kids with its three small upstairs bedrooms. The three boys eagerly took the wood-floor bedroom, with their bunk bed on the right side of the room and a single bed tucked nicely under the sloped ceiling on the left. Our daughter Desiree adored the light blue room with a teddy bear border and soft blue carpet. Next, Jim and I moved into the more oversized master bedroom, with a small en-suite bathroom in the far corner.

Walking through the back door, you found yourself standing in the panel-wainscoting dining room with dark wallpaper. Straight ahead was a short hall that held our few coat hooks before reaching the front door. To your right was a larger galley-type kitchen with a fridge, small counter with ceramic-built-in type antique sink, and stove. To your left was the washer and dryer first, then a tall archway to the playroom, and our microwave stood sheepishly at the end.

How Do You House a Large Family?

Downstairs were beautiful high ceilings. Deep window wells were found throughout the house. The playroom was hard to miss with its bright pink walls and the old white wainscoting. A three-piece bathroom was in the corner of this playroom, making it L- shaped but convenient for our young children. The light grey carpets in the playroom ran through the hall (up the stairs) and into the living room. The grey living room was just big enough to hold our oversized, brown corduroy sectional couch, not leaving much room for anything else. It didn't match, but it was cozy, and we enjoyed it.

Our first change was the L-shaped church pew that we'd brought into our small dining room. This new addition helped us slide more kids around the table without using more bulky chairs. But, as you know, our family grew. One by one, three more cute girls arrived, and the small girls' room became increasingly crowded.

I remember one dark night when we heard the baby crying across the hall from our room. My loving husband exited the cozy, warm bed and crossed the hall to the girls' room. By the moon's light, he entered their room, bunk bed on his left with a wooden ladder reaching out to the single bed on his right. Stepping over the wooden ladder, he reached the crying baby. After settling her, he turned and, looking forward to his warm bed, forgot the bunk bed ladder, painfully stubbing his big toe. A muffled cry came from the girls' room, and I heard, more than I saw, Jim hobbling slowly back to bed. This was the painful night Jim decided something had to be done, even if it meant giving up his master bedroom! Soon the downstairs playroom and the bathroom were made into our master bedroom. The archway to the kitchen was closed off, and the bright pink walls were painted forest green. The upstairs master bedroom, per the girls' insistent instruction, was painted pink and purple, while their teddy bear bedroom across the hall turned into the messy, out-of-the-way playroom.

In 2003, another blessing was on the way, and the bedrooms were quite full. Because of our newly expected addition, the hunt for a bigger house began.

"We're looking for a starter home for eight kids," we informed our real estate agent friend.

"I don't think there is such a thing," she stated skeptically.

"Lord, how can we afford a bigger house on one income while feeding eight growing children?" we asked.

Our rent at that point was affordable. Even buying a small house no bigger than our beautiful stone house would probably double what we paid in rent.

"Lord, what is your plan for us?" we asked as we continued to look and fervently pray.

Finally, with the help of our representative, we found a house on four acres, with a small barn, in an out-of-the-way town. We could make it work, couldn't we? We put in an offer we could afford and continued praying. It was declined. We knew we couldn't offer more. Believing this was not where God wanted us to be was hard. We continued looking, praying for peace in the whole situation.

A few months later, we heard that church friends of ours were moving to England for work, and they were thinking of selling their big house. Jim and I looked at each other with raised eyebrows and big smiles. We had been to this old house (a two-room schoolhouse), and it was huge! The original school room had been made into a dining room that was twenty-five feet by nineteen feet, with a ceiling thirteen feet high. It also had a large and small bathroom, a good-sized kitchen, and a bedroom with lowered ceilings. The second school room had been made into a living room, thirty feet by twenty feet, with ceilings twelve feet high and two bedrooms with dropped ceilings. We promptly set up a time to visit and discuss the possibilities.

It didn't take much thought to know that this was where we needed to be. So we made all the arrangements to purchase the

How Do You House a Large Family?

schoolhouse, and we hesitantly notified our landlady of our move. Upon hearing this, she decided to auction the rental house and its original one hundred acres.

On the day of the auction, we arrived at our empty house, full of memories, to see what would become of it. As we walked through what felt like countless people in the back yard, we couldn't help but smile at the conversations we overheard.

"Did you hear that there was a big family living in the house?"

"Yah! They had something like ten kids!" I wanted to interject into the crowd, "No, it was only eight."

"That house is so small. How did they all fit in there?" another voice questioned. Jim and I smiled tenderly at each other as we made our way to the house.

Upon entering, we met our landlady, who smiled and greeted us warmly. After a short conversation, Jim told her how much we enjoyed living there but how it was too small for our growing family.

"You should have told me. You guys were great tenants. I would have put an addition on for you," she declared.

With mixed feelings, we left after the property didn't sell for the reserved bid.

During the first week at our new house, the kids spent their days playing in the laundry room/office, as it was the smallest room. There seemed to be just too much room for them in the rest of the house. But slowly, over time, they made their way out of the laundry room, and so did all their many toys! Our oldest daughter, Desiree, even started telling people she was going to boarding school! I guess that's one way to explain that you live in an old schoolhouse and homeschool.

Why did we ever waver in our trust in God? He supplied us with this huge, special, old schoolhouse at a starter home price. God is good all the time!

Family at Large

You know you have a large family when ...

- *You move into a new town and you double the population. Neighbours discuss changing the blue sign on the edge of town to reflect the new population.*
- *Your children don't even bother asking for souvenirs from an attraction. They're just thankful you brought them.*
- *Your fridge is set colder than normal to accommodate the number of times the door is opened in a day.*
- *Your family goes away for a day, and when you return, everything in the fridge is frozen because not enough people opened the fridge that day.*
- *Every form you have to fill out is an L-O-N-G form. I was filling out the census form, and Jim asked if it was the long form. To which I responded, "Every form we fill out is a long-form."*

Six
Answered Prayer

"And my God will meet all your needs according to the riches of his glory in Christ Jesus."
(Philippians 4:19)

THREE MONTHS BEFORE Melissa, our eighth child, was born, Jim noticed a bump behind my right ear, quite by accident. I have a shoulder-length, feathered-back hairstyle, and my blonde hair on the right side kept sticking out. He would gently push it back down, but over time, he realized the problem was my lumpy head, not my hair. No one else seemed to notice it except him.

My family doctor thought this lumpy head was related to some extra fatty tissue, so he sent me to a plastic surgeon. Four months later, I finally received an appointment. Twelve-year-old Desiree came with me to care for baby Melissa, who was now approaching six weeks old. Thirteen-year-old Derek stayed home to babysit the other five. After I arrived, the nurse proceeded to scare me by having me sign papers for surgery. I thought I was there to talk to a doctor. Nevertheless, by the time I left, I'd already had a needle biopsy.

I planned to take the kids camping with my siblings and their families that same day. Unfortunately, Jim could only camp with us for the weekend, so I'd be on my own. During this time, I struggled inwardly with what was going on. Furthermore, I was fighting the wet, rainy weather with eight children and three tents. Finally, I admitted to myself, "I am *no* super mom!" and departed early.

At home, I found out that my lump wasn't fatty tissue after all. The doctor's office scheduled me for an incision biopsy two weeks later.

Jim was beside me during the incision biopsy, with little Melissa in his strong arms. The doctor informed us he found nothing unusual.

"Do I have the right side?" the doctor asked aloud, simultaneously making me both happy and scared. Maybe I was just a lumpy person.

After I had a Tylenol 3, Jim went back to work. I had to bring Derek to meet the Cadets at church for the annual Cadet camping—tears were close to brimming over while I attempted to keep my neck hidden. I didn't want to talk to just anyone about it. When Derek was settled and on his way, I drove off to visit a close friend.

Later, we were informed that nothing was found during the biopsy. I didn't have much time to think of all the "could bes" and "what ifs" because, during the month of August, we also moved to a new house—one load at a time. Each morning I would fill the twelve-passenger van and utility trailer, get the kids buckled in, and drive ten minutes to our new house. Then we would unload and clean for the day.

I was scheduled for a 3-D X-ray or an MRI on Tuesday, September 16, at 11:30. On that unforgettable day, Jim and I gathered baby Melissa and two-year-old Elizabeth to take them with us to the University Hospital in London, Ontario. I nursed Melissa one more time, hoping to fill her up before the MRI so that she'd be content for Jim. A nurse approached and informed me that I'd

Answered Prayer

receive a dye in my blood system; therefore, I couldn't nurse for forty-eight hours. Panic began to rise within me. I had never tried a bottle with Melissa. In fact, I hadn't tried a bottle since my first child thirteen years earlier. Jim reassured me that it would be okay and we'd pick up the formula on the way home.

As I slowly entered the large torpedo chamber lying on my back, they informed me that the test would take about an hour. I began praying for my husband, my children, and others as they entered my mind. During this time, the hydro went off, and they had to restart the machine. Since having eight children, my lower back wasn't strong. Lying flat on my back was very painful when done for extended periods. After they finally pulled me out an hour and a half later to give me the dye and finish the test, I was in great pain. I couldn't lie down any longer. I needed help getting off the table and could barely walk. They tried to persuade me to take the dye so that they could continue the scan, but I said no, I could take no more. The tears streamed down my cheeks! Finally, they reluctantly agreed to go on with what they had, and I painfully left to nurse my baby.

Two weeks later, on Thursday, October 2, I received a phone call from the neurosurgeon's office with an appointment for that coming Monday, October 6 (a day before our fourteenth anniversary).

"The MRI showed that you have a tumour on your spine," she stated.

My brain worked in slow motion. *Tumour*! How big was it? The size of a marble or golf ball, maybe? It was on my spine? What did this all mean? I hung up the phone. Do I call someone? Jim, of course, but what do I tell him? Or should I wait till he gets home? I was in a daze for about half an hour. Reluctantly, I picked up the phone and called Jim at work. I told him about the call and then asked him to try to get Monday off to come with me. As we said goodbye, I started to get emotional while he reassured me that he'd be there for me. My parents still knew nothing of what was happening, but I couldn't call them. I reasoned that we didn't know anything for sure, so why worry them about it? They were so busy with their own business. Living two hours away, it wasn't like they could just come over and visit. So I decided to wait.

When Jim arrived home that night, he asked me if I'd called my parents. He strongly felt I should tell them, but I wasn't ready yet. By the next day, Saturday, my husband more or less ordered me to call my parents. Helplessly, I entered our home office and quietly closed the door behind me. I dialed, anxiously waiting, my stomach doing a flip-flop when my mother finally picked up the phone.

"Is Dad close by? I have to talk to both of you," I began.

"Well, he's in the car. We were going out; I'll get him and be right back," she answered.

I knew she could tell this was serious. Soon they were both on the phone, and I explained everything as briefly as possible. I didn't want to worry them unnecessarily.

"What time is your appointment and where? We'll meet you there!" came the reply. "We can watch Melissa for you while you and Jim talk to the doctor."

Their response took me by surprise. My emotions started to run wild again. I knew I would turn into a basket case if my mom were there. Did I really want them at the appointment? Was I strong enough to keep my tears at bay? I told Jim to keep me busy all weekend so that I wouldn't overthink. That Sunday night was one of the hardest nights of my life. We lay in each other's arms, crying, talking, and praying. We shared our joys and fears and then gave it all to the Lord. Finally, in the wee hours of the morning, I fell into a peaceful sleep.

University Hospital was its usual busy self, and I felt small in its busyness. The butterflies in my stomach threatened to carry me away. My parents were nowhere to be found as we continued to the tenth floor to see my neurologist, Dr. Ng, for the first time. We—Jim, Melissa, and I—waited in the waiting room for only three minutes before a nurse led us to an examination room, which we had passed on our way in. Jim and I quietly talked as we waited for the doctor. We were trying to keep our hearts light. Mom and Dad walked by a short time later, peeking in the open door as they heard our voices. Jim passed Melissa to them. He then pointed to the chairs farther down, where they could sit and wait. I sensed my mom would also break down if she talked too much. Therefore, little was said, while I sent up a short prayer of thanksgiving. Minutes later, Dr. Ng arrived and asked me the following questions.

"Any problems hearing?"

"No."

"Any problems with your sight?"

"No."

"Any headaches?"

"No."

"How did you end up here if you had no side effects?" he questioned.

We explained the whole hair-sticking-out story. He was very interested and explained that I had a tumour near the base of my brain.

"Follow me, and I'll show you the MRI," he announced.

We followed him to where my parents sat and then turned right. On our left was a long, lighted box with X-ray pictures on it. Dr. Ng realized we had passed my parents, so he invited them to join us. So the five of us huddled close to one specific X-ray picture.

"You have to think of your head as a loaf of bread," he educated us. "First, we're slicing it from left to right, starting at the top of your head and going to your neck. Then we did it again, only this time from top to bottom, going from your left ear to your right ear."

As we looked at the pictures, he explained that the top of my brain was fine, but as we moved down to the top of my right ear, the tumour started between my spine and brain. The further we went down the x-rays, the bigger and broader the tumour became.

Finally, close to the bottom of my left ear, you could see it starting on the left side of my spine. Boy, was my head lopsided! Jim and I couldn't get over how far the tumour had pushed the back right side of my head. At that time, I guessed the tumour took up one-sixth of my head. Later my parents and Jim said more like one-third! The doctor informed us that if moulded into a ball, it would be the size of a baseball!

I was then escorted back to the examination room, where the doctor did a series of balance, strength, hearing, and seeing tests. Dr. Ng called Jim to join us, announcing that the tumour had to come out, even though it wasn't causing any problems. He figured it had been there for five to ten years and didn't see why I couldn't finish nursing Melissa first.

"She needs you now! We will wait," stated Dr. Ng.

"How do you know it's not cancerous?" Jim asked. "The needle biopsy didn't go in very deep, and I was there when they did the incision biopsy. He didn't go that deep either! So how can you be sure?"

He looked back in his notes and found no evidence showing sufficient tests were done.

"Yes, I think I would agree with you. We will schedule a CAT scan biopsy. They can see the tumour and take a sample from it. Is that okay with you?"

Yes, this was good. First, we filled out more paperwork. Mom and Dad then took us out for coffee to talk. We all felt eager for the next step, encouraged by the doctor, and amazed at the size of the tumour.

After our coffee, I dropped Jim off at work and stopped at our pastor's house. I knew I could no longer keep this a secret. I needed prayer warriors. Finding my pastor at home, I explained my situation to him, requesting prayer from our church family. I also asked not to mention possible cancer because I didn't want to scare my children. We spent some time in prayer before I headed home to explain to my eight children what was to take place soon. Then, with peace in my heart and a smile on my face, I began to explain how MRIs work.

"It was so *cool*!" I began.

"Your head is a loaf of bread?" one replied.

I felt strength I never thought possible as I explained to them everything I knew, purposely leaving out any "what ifs." Right now, we were living with facts. Mom had a large tumour. It had to come out. I thanked the Lord again for no side effects. The Lord knew my kids had to see me as the same old mom doing the same old things. It would have been much harder if I had been sick or had other visible effects. I also told the kids that their friends might start talking about Mom and possibly saying scary or untrue things.

"Who would know more about Mom—your friends, or Mom and Dad?" I quizzed.

We then encouraged them to talk to us if they had any questions or concerns.

The following Wednesday, October 15, at 9:30 AM, I was scheduled for my CAT scan biopsy. Physically I could feel the prayers as I entered the hospital with Jim and Melissa (who were the big attraction or distraction). I was once again filling out papers and nursing Melissa simultaneously. This time I was thankful, as they had me lie on my left side instead of my back. Next, my head was strapped into a head clamp so I wouldn't move. They used the incision biopsy scar as a guide and began the scan. The health care team informed me that the needles couldn't penetrate the tumour. Because of this, the specialist felt very sure it was a non-cancerous tumour. Once again, they couldn't properly collect enough tissue to diagnose the tumour.

After a couple of weeks, on October 27, I could no longer wait. Melissa was five months old, and my heart was heavy with overstimulated thoughts.

"All our children need a mom," Jim reassured. "Book the MRI with dye so we can schedule surgery."

The doctor's office called back a few days later with my MRI date and time. This was scheduled for Monday, November 10, at 9:30 A.M. The next step was getting Melissa on the bottle. I tried four types of bottles and nipples, but she would drink nothing. She wouldn't even accept the breast milk I pumped. She would cry and cry till we were both crying. She won. I nursed her. Every day at 10:00 AM, you could hear crying from both of us. Jim would try at night, and my friends during the day. Still, she wouldn't take a bottle. A friend offered to breastfeed her for the three days I had the dye in my system. I was shocked, to say the least, but lost for what else to do. I didn't want my baby to go hungry. On the evening of Friday, November 7, three days before my MRI and still breastfeeding, I took one last measure. I emailed everyone I could think of to pray that she would take the bottle. Saturday at 10:00 AM, I sat down and took a deep breath, preparing myself against the screams. She clasped the bottle in her hands, brought it to her mouth, and drank like she'd been doing this for months. I cried tears of joy as I thanked God for yet another little miracle.

That Sunday, November 9, began another difficult night. During our 7:00 PM evening church service, I stayed in the nursery with Melissa and nursed her. I was trying to prepare myself for after the service. Joanne Puklicz, another friend and mother of seven, was taking my baby for a few days so that I wouldn't be tempted to nurse her after the MRI.

I now understood the terrible pain young moms must go through when they choose to give up their babies for adoption. It truly is a selfless love. "This is just too hard! God give me strength!" I prayed that night.

After nursing her that one last time, I put Melissa in her car seat, and she started crying. I prayed harder for strength, but the tears started burning my eyes. Joanne saw that I wasn't handling this very well. She quietly took Melissa from me and smiled as she turned and left the room. Jim drew me close and held me tight as I cried. We waited a few minutes to give the Pukliczs a chance to go and for me to gain my composure. Then we gravely started for home.

On the way home, Desiree and Elizabeth cried along with me. Everyone else was *very* quiet. I tried to console Elizabeth and find out why she was crying.

"Let her cry; it's a sad night," Jim said in a broken-hearted voice.

About an hour later, when the kids were in bed, I began to gain composure. The phone rang, and Jim answered and said another homeschooler wanted to speak to me. She was in tears. She'd just heard my story and offered to breastfeed Melissa. I then explained my evening and thanked her for her amazing offer. I admire these people who would help out in such a sacrificial way. I don't think I could ever do that.

The following day we left early after Jim's mom arrived to watch our other kids. This MRI went much better. I explained what happened last time, and they said I could move around as long as I was still after the knocking started, a sign that the machine was running. This time the hydro stayed on, so thankfully we didn't have to start all over again. *Yeah*!

Despite the pumping, my chest continued to be very sore for the next few days. I couldn't believe it. My milk was a bluish colour! Joanne had phoned Monday night to tell me Melissa was fine, just mad because she wanted her mom. She was thankfully doing well with the bottle. It was so good to talk to her. By Wednesday morning, Melissa was home. What a day of rejoicing!

We had to meet with Dr. Ng again the following Thursday, November 20, at 12:45 PM. I dropped the kids off with another homeschooling friend. Then I went to pick up Jim from work. Together, we received more details about how the surgery would go. He also informed us that the large artery he had been concerned about was not close to the tumour. It looked very close to us. I suppose millimeters are miles to a surgeon! He sounded very confident, and that made us feel more at ease. He also informed us that I would have an indentation where the tumour was in my head. The tumour had worn muscles down that would never return. Later that week, his receptionist called us with a surgery date of January 9, 2004.

Christmas was "interesting," as there were times when it was faith-strengthening and other times when I was apprehensive. We prayed diligently, wondering what the Lord had in mind for us in the coming year. Our parents and my godparents spoke freely with Jim and me about it. Talking about it lifted my soul, continuously reminding me (and others) how God was still working in my life.

On Monday, December 29, at 2:00 PM, my mom met me at the pre-admission clinic at University Hospital. We had an enjoyable day out, especially since my mom lived two hours away and we hadn't spent much time together, just the two of us, since I got married. Even when we did visit them, small children often demanded our time. My mom commented on how she was finding out so much about me again!

Well, I was weighed in, and then all the paperwork started. There was much information shared that day! The nurse told me that I wouldn't be able to eat anything from midnight the night before surgery, as it was scheduled for 8:00 AM. I'd have to be there at 6:00 AM. I was thankful to hear that I was scheduled as the day's first appointment!

Only two people would be allowed in the surgery waiting room during my surgery. Mom made me giggle when, without hesitation, she announced it would be her and Jim. She said she would figure out later how to tell Dad that he couldn't be there. Here they informed me that they were treating this as back surgery. I would stay in the hospital for three to four days. I wouldn't be able to lift anything over ten pounds for six weeks, and this included Melissa. At six weeks, I'd go for a checkup, and they'd decide whether or not to extend my "no lifting or doing anything" to ten or twelve weeks. During this time, I wouldn't be able to drive, and the list of "do nots" went on and on. Listening to the nurse made me feel useless. I was a go-go person. How would I ever sit still for two weeks, let alone two months?

I prepared about a week-and-a-half worth of meals for my freezer to fill my days. Trying to get my kids ahead in school was also a priority for me, since I spent a lot of time homeschooling. I prepared homeschooling lessons for Jim to teach for the next six weeks. The kids were packed, and my house was spotless. Now I was ready. Or was I? What if something happened to me? What if I was different after all of this? What would they remember about me? Many days were spent worrying about my family, even though I tried not to think about it. During this time, I also wrote each of my children a personal letter, telling them things I admired about them and also sharing encouraging words for the future.

Thursday, January 8, arrived, and Jim began his parental leave. In the morning, he took some of the little girls with him and went to apply. (They had told us to come with the kids, and he would get through the line faster!) We had a nice lunch all together and then said our goodbyes. Jim made a round trip, dropping the younger five kids off here and there at family and friends.

Meanwhile, I stayed home and called the doctor's office as instructed to ensure my surgery time was still scheduled for 8:00 AM the next day. Dr. Ng's secretary informed me that my surgery had been moved to 2:00 PM. Disappointed, I asked about the time change. She told me that I was still the only one on for the day. All his other patients who had an appointment that day had been cancelled. This made me realize that the Lord had His hand in this. I said another prayer of thanksgiving.

Family at Large

After a small dinner that evening, Jim brought Desiree to visit her friends. Then Jim and I brought Derek and Victoria to other friends. We stayed and visited awhile to pass the time. Even though we got home that night after 10:00 PM, we still stayed up to watch the movie *It's My Home School, and I Will Cry if I Want To!* It was so good to laugh together. After that, we—or should I say, I—ate lots of donuts and anything else I could get my hands on. I wanted to fill up before midnight, and boy, was I full.

The following day we tried our hardest to sleep late. Even though the house was quiet with only the two of us, our bodies told us it was time to wake up. We lay there for a while looking at the ceiling and talking, but by 9:00 AM, we'd had enough! I told Jim to eat breakfast while I was in the shower so that I didn't have to watch him. He said that he was fasting on my behalf!

"Don't be silly," I laughed.

"I won't eat anything until this is over and I know you're okay. Now go take your shower," he stated.

I gave him a sad smile, told him he didn't have to, and then hesitantly left to shower. We were all ready around 10:00 AM and still had another hour and a half left before leaving. So I busied myself with putting away clean laundry and tidying the girls' room and then the boys'. Meanwhile, Jim was pacing here and there.

"How can you do that?" he finally said in frustration.

"Do what?"

"How can you be so calm?" he replied with a stressed look.

I hugged him and said I keep busy to stay calm, so I don't think about it. A few minutes later, he found me in our room. I had been straightening up the room when a flood of doubt and worry came over me, and the tears began to roll. Jim came in and held me. We prayed for the surgeon and all the others who would be helping with the surgery. We prayed for our family and the days ahead, asking the Lord to help us accept whatever His plan was for our lives and to give us peace in our hearts so we could witness to others through this. We both left that room with peaceful hearts, feeling everything would be okay.

We took our time to get to University Hospital. Both of us talked very little. When we did talk, it was mostly funny things, things in our past, and happy memories. At the hospital, we made our way to the pre-admit clinic again to get papers and directions on where to go next. As we left, my mom and dad met us in the hall. I hugged my dad and told him I loved him, thinking he would be waiting in the front lobby. It didn't take long before I had to go, and the tears started flowing again. Jim quietly led me to our next stop, expecting my mom to follow.

Now I had to get ready for surgery. I was privileged to model the newest look in blue hospital gowns with really cool white stockings. The stockings were to keep the circulation moving in my legs while I was in surgery.

"So why have you come to visit us today, Mrs. Schreuders?" asked the nurse in a fun tone.

"I am here to get sick!" I replied with a smile.

I went on to explain that I had experienced no side effects with my tumour. We continued to joke around and have a great time. Once my IV was in, she asked if anyone was at the hospital waiting for me. She then proceeded to fetch Jim for me. Before I knew it, they had also let my parents (both of them) sit with me. I was in better humour then, and I think I had the jolly nurse to thank for that. I had the feeling this would be fun—if I let it. Two o'clock came, when they came to take me upstairs to prep for surgery. Apparently, I was not "preppy" enough. Then off I went for a "taxi ride" down the hall and up the elevator. Within minutes we were at a hall, where Jim was informed that he could go no further. We said our goodbyes and I love yous. Would I see him again? I suddenly wondered and began to pray fervently.

"Lord, I need you now. I feel so alone and scared. Lord, show me that you're here. I need you, Lord." I bit my lower lip to fight at the tears as my bed was being turned right into another waiting room. There were four beds to the right and three to the left of me.

"Joanne! How are you? What a coincidence that you're here today too," said a familiar voice.

"Sue! What are you doing in here?" I answered while praying a quick prayer of thanks to the Lord, who knew just what I needed.

Sue and her family used to be part of our church family. The previous year she'd been our real estate agent before we bought our schoolhouse privately. As we continued our pleasant visit, she explained that she was awaiting knee surgery.

A nurse came to check on me, and I realized I still had my glasses on. So I asked if she could give them to Jim in the waiting room. She hesitated a moment before looking cautiously around.

"I'll get him so he can wait here with you till you go into surgery," the nurse whispered with a smile.

I probably said thank you ten times, if not more. Jim was beaming from ear to ear as he quietly entered the room. He greeted Sue and told us he and her husband had been talking in the waiting room. Jim's prayer was also answered, giving him someone else to talk to in the waiting room. As we sat there, we realized that someone was being sent home. How disappointing to be prepped and ready for surgery only to be sent home.

The anesthesiologist came to introduce himself and see if I was allergic to anything. He asked a few questions and then continued on his way. We suddenly witnessed another gentleman two beds down being sent home. He was waiting for bypass surgery for the second time! He was not happy but had no choice. There weren't enough beds in the intensive care unit. The surgeon apologized; you could see he felt terrible for this frustrated gentleman. Jim and I looked at each other and, in that glance, asked each other, "Are we going home too?"

Dr. Ng's assistant, the resident doctor, introduced himself and asked some questions. Then he explained how they would shave

Answered Prayer

the back of my head before making an incision from midway down my head to my neck.

"Do you have a hairdresser's license for that?" Jim asked in a serious tone.

"Uh no?" hesitantly responded the resident doctor, not knowing if Jim was serious.

"He likes my hair long. He would like it longer," I informed the doctor, trying to set his mind at ease.

Jim and the doctor agreed it wouldn't be shaved off, just a strip down the middle, an inverted Mohawk. I would have preferred it shaved so that it could all grow together, but who am I to argue with my doctor and husband? Since the tumour wasn't connected to anything, they should be able to go in and pop it out, he joked. He assured us it wouldn't be much longer.

By three o'clock that afternoon, I kissed my husband yet again before I was wheeled down a long hall. I felt more at peace this time, for I knew the Lord was there holding my hand. I calmly chatted with the nurse as she guided me to the operating room.

"Will you be there for the surgery?" I asked.

"I'll be there for part of it. Why?" she responded.

"I just want to make sure that my feet stay warm. When I wake up, I want my feet to be warm."

"Okay!" she stated with a smile in her voice as we rolled through the door of the operating room.

Then she announced to all in the room, "We have a real woman here! She wants warm blankets on her feet!" Feeling a slight colour rise in my cheeks, I went along with the banter as she introduced everyone to me.

"The ladies over there are Mary and Jill," she said, pointing to my left.

"I would say nice to see you, but I don't have my glasses," I joked.

"That's okay," stated Mary, "I'm the skinny one!" Everyone joined in the laughter.

The last thing I remember before going to sleep is the doctor announcing to everyone, "She has eight children! She doesn't look like she has eight children!" I then took a short nap with a smile and a prayer in my heart. (At least, for me, it seemed like a quick nap.)

I faintly heard my name being called from far away. I tried to lift open my groggy eyelids, but they seemed lined with lead. My shoulders, neck, and head were aching, and my thoughts were jumbled. Thank you, Lord, for warm feet! The doctor was there; I could hear him talking to me, saying something. My strained ears listened to the word "everything" and "fine." I tried deciphering his words again, but my brain felt thick and heavy. Soon I could open my eyes, but nothing was clear. I didn't have my glasses yet. My "taxi ride" was here, and I was now on the move again. I wanted to see Jim so bad. I didn't want him to worry anymore. I was here and fine, except for this headache! The gentleman pushing my bed stopped for a second.

"Sir, you can't come this way. You have to go to her room and wait there," he stated. I could vaguely hear Jim's voice. Where are my glasses when I need them? I couldn't see him. Where was he? We slowly started moving again. After a short elevator ride, I arrived at my new room. They got me settled and began explaining my situation to me. I had a vacuum-pac coming out of my incision in the back of my head to suck out any internal bleeding. It didn't hurt a lot; it just ached. And my neck and shoulders had taut muscles. I was weak but more awake by this time and eager to see Jim and my parents. They slowly approached from behind the curtain. I could tell they were all worried, but I still couldn't see them clearly.

"You had a hamburger with onions, didn't you?" I jokingly questioned my mom, recalling a previous surgery I had when I was younger.

Answered Prayer

At that time my mom had come to me, the same as now, smelling of hamburgers and onions. Unfortunately, they didn't see the humour in this statement tonight, and Jim got even edgier.

"I told you we shouldn't have gone out to eat!" Jim tensely announced.

I tried to reassure him that I was joking, but it wasn't working. After a short time, my parents left, and Jim stayed longer. He told me briefly what had happened. I left at 3:00 PM for surgery, and the doctor didn't call Jim until 7:00 PM. My two to three-hour surgery had taken four hours! My parents dragged Jim out of the hospital to get him to eat something, promising they would return within half an hour. Waiting around again until 8:30, he started to panic. He returned to the operating hall, knowing he shouldn't go down there, and asked a passing nurse to see if I was there and okay. The nurse returned to inform Jim that I was fine and that he should wait for me upstairs, as I would be there shortly. Later I apologized for forgetting to tell him that I'd taken forever to come out of the anesthetic during my last surgery. Well, apparently he didn't go upstairs; he waited right there for about another half hour. This is when he saw me, and I couldn't see him. He recalled the tubes coming out of my head, which certainly scared him. Running upstairs, he excitedly told my parents that I was on my way to the room. Again, he was stopped and informed that he wasn't allowed in until I was settled. It wasn't until about 10:00 PM that he finally saw me again. After about an hour's visit, Jim made his long, slow way home in a snowstorm to let the children know I was all right.

That night I wasn't allowed to sleep peacefully. The nurses woke me up every fifteen to twenty minutes to do exercises. First, I'd have to hold out my arm, and the nurse would gently but firmly push down on my hand, and I would have to push back. My legs were next, and then we moved to the other arm. Even though I took Gravol and pain pills, the queasiness and neck pain remained constant. Prayer and rest helped keep the tension in my sore neck and shoulders minimal.

The following day, Mom and Dad surprised me with another short visit. They had stayed at a local hotel overnight and showed up for a quick stop before picking up Victoria and Christina, who had been staying with Jim's parents. Just before they left, Dr. Ng's assistant came to check on me and informed me that the tumour had surrounded two nerves, which they hadn't expected. This resulted in removing a part of a nerve to get the tumour out. As they were closing up, I started to bleed excessively. They had to reopen the incision to stop the bleeding. He then assured me that they had extracted the whole tumour. He was pretty sure it was non-cancerous but informed us it was being sent to the lab to confirm its diagnosis. After a few more questions, he continued on his morning rounds. My parents left shortly after that, and I eagerly awaited Jim's return.

Jim and I had a pleasant visit that day, including a real bathroom break late morning with the nurse's approval. That night was extremely tough, as I became a not-so-happy camper due to muscle spasms in my neck. This was followed by difficulty getting a nurse to assist me when I needed to turn to a more comfortable position.

Sunday arrived with the resident doctor and more questions. This is when it finally sunk in that I would never feel the right side of the back of my head again. They cut the nerves for skin sensation from behind my right ear to the centre back of my head. This resulted in an annoying tingly sensation, like the kind you get at the dentist after the freezing comes out. I prayed it would go away soon. He also showed me kindness by removing the tube from my head. Furthermore, he informed me I could go home Monday if I felt up to it.

Next, the nurse helped me get cleaned up. I was amazed to hear that they have these new shower caps that are water-free.

They warm them in a microwave, then put them on your head and massage your hair. I don't understand how they work, but I was thankful they did a good job removing most of the blood in my hair and improving my bedhead. I felt more like a human again! At this point, I started walking the halls a little. I heard about a young man who was in because of a diving accident. The lady in the bed next to me probably wouldn't make it. As I looked at all the pictures of awards being presented to the doctors for brain surgery, it started to sink in how serious my situation was.

Later that afternoon, Jim and I walked to the cafeteria with the nurse's permission. I felt the need to get out, and a trip to the cafeteria seemed the best place to go. Jim remained slightly worried, but I smiled, letting him know I had been up and down the halls enough times. I was looking for more of an adventure. So we slowly made our way down to the cafeteria, Jim and I, arm in arm, followed by many stares.

"Look at that lady in the pajamas and the big bandage on the back of her head!"

"I wonder what happened to her?"

I sat briefly and then asked Jim to eat his muffin a little faster. I felt cramping in my shoulders from trying to hold my head up. I knew I had to get back to my relaxing bed soon.

The next day was my final day at the hospital. I had a shower and got all ready to go. Jim didn't arrive soon enough. I said my goodbyes, and then Jim carefully helped me to the car. He had brought all sorts of pillows for me to lie on in the vehicle's back seat. I smiled as I wondered if there would be enough room for me! My stomach was starting to feel a little queasy again.

"Lord, please help me get home without hurling," I prayed. The Lord was gracious, as I fell into a light sleep, waking up close to home. Boy, did it feel good to be home.

The following days I lay around and let Jim be my manservant. Jim arranged a visitor for me every day, keeping me busy for the short time I could stay awake in the afternoon. I enjoyed watching the shocked look on people's faces when I answered the door. I felt I had to keep moving or I'd slowly seize up. So I would walk a little and then lie back down again. What surprised me most was how much work it was to eat. I never really realized how many neck muscles you use when you chew. Because of this, I ate small portions at a time, usually only eating for less than fifteen-minute stretches before needing a break. My sense of balance was also skewed, so I stayed close to solid pieces of furniture. The nights were long and always included a few walking times. These times of walking around helped keep the muscles in my shoulders loose and were more enjoyable when Jim kept me company while feeding Melissa her bottle.

As expected, Desiree returned home first. She couldn't stand being away from home any longer. What a great help she was to Jim. Melissa also came home sooner because Jim couldn't live without his baby. I, on the other hand, hadn't been looking forward to seeing my baby. Don't get me wrong—I loved my baby. It was knowing the heartache I would experience at being unable to hold her. Therefore, once she was there, Jim put pillows all around me and gently laid my baby in my securely supported arms. There I sat, crying and kissing my baby girl. That is when I knew the time away had been way too long. By Thursday night, we were all home together again. Thank the Lord!

Elizabeth, who was two years old, loved to ask questions about Mom's surgery.

"Mom? Did the doctor give you a haircut? Did the doctor cut you and take out your tumour? Did he put the zipper in?" Jim had measured my incision to be five inches long. I had eighteen staples holding the incision together, creating a zippered look. I joked with Jim, saying I should put some sticky, wiggly eyes on the back of my head where I was shaved. That way, the kids would know that mom *does* have eyes in the back of her head! Desiree told me the incision made her feel sick to her stomach. Nicolas and Vicky agreed with her, but Nathan, who was nine years old, thought it was pretty cool. I kept noticing him sneaking up behind me, secretly checking out my zipper for the two weeks I had it. The others quietly stood by, scared for Mom but happy to know her fat face would return to the same size they remembered.

Soon we found a comfortable way that Melissa could safely sit with me, as long as someone was there. One evening, early on, we found out I couldn't hold her for long, even with securely supported arms. The strain on my neck and shoulders would become unbearable. This night, we had been forgotten, and no one heard me call. We were both in tears when we were found twenty minutes later.

During this time, I also learned that no matter how organized you are, there will still be those moments of crisis.

"Where's the toilet paper?" someone screamed.

We had just moved four months before the surgery, and I had bought extra supplies to fill all the new cupboards. Now Jim would only be responsible for purchasing milk and bread, or so I thought! Unfortunately, I missed an important step: telling them where I put everything. Constantly, I was asked, "Mom, where is this? Mom, where is that?" I sure could have used earplugs some days. I thought, *Whatever happened to Mom having six weeks of peace and quiet?*

During the months before surgery, I had also planned school for the six weeks Jim would be our kids' substitute teacher. I meticulously wrote everything out so the kids' education would not suffer. Education was important to me, but was it more important than the time I could have spent with my kids before surgery? What if something had gone wrong?

As I lay on the couch in the living room, I could hear Jim teaching the kids in the dining room. Ten minutes after they started, they came running through the living room. Heading for the mudroom, they started pulling on their coats and boots.

"Where are you guys going?" I questioned.

"Dad says we can have recess!" came the happy reply.

As I lay there helpless, I realized this was Jim's time with his children, a time for them to get to know each other and create memorable bonds. Schooling could come later.

I visited a physiotherapist twice, and she showed me exercises to do at home. I learned fast that if I did my exercises, I wouldn't get painful muscle spasms and would hopefully recover more quickly. By four weeks, I was helping teach the kids again. Sadly, I couldn't do it for long, as I would tire fast. I found out about the same time that I had low iron, which explained the tiredness. By six weeks, I was pretty well on my way, happy to hear Dr. Ng tell me I could resume life as long as I listened to my body and didn't push myself. I continued with iron pills for about six months before my levels returned to normal. Another MRI was scheduled for February 16, 2005, to ensure nothing had returned.

Generous people called wanting to help, so we suggested freezer meals. Well, when the Lord answered this prayer, he responded hugely. We received approximately forty meals, plus baking. At one point, I speculated they would stop, and then we could begin to place a dent in the freezer meals I had made. However, the Lord knew we were working off Jim's one parental leave income, so He kept blessing us with an abundance! What an awesome God!

We wanted to show the kids how awesome our God was, so Jim started hanging up all the cards we received on a string across the kitchen. Soon that string became two, and in the end, we had three lines with cards on them. Derek commented, "The whole world must be praying for us!"

Being the homeschooling mom I am, and taking every teachable moment, I took out the world map and pointed out the

Answered Prayer

different places where the cards came from. We had friends in Africa who had their friends praying for us. The kids' eyes grew as we pointed out our friends in Alberta, the United States, Holland, and all over Ontario. These friends would each share our story with others, who would also pray. Even I was shocked to see how much of our world *was* praying for us!

Today I still tend to feel the crummy weather distinctly in my neck and shoulders. Often it will stiffen up on me on those damp days. The key I've found is remembering my exercises, and then off I go again. I thank the Lord for allowing me to visit with my family and friends for just a little longer here on earth before I have the honour of living with Him forever.

You know you have a large family when ...
- *The family dog doesn't need a doggie door because enough people are going in and out to accommodate him.*
- *Your two-year-old says, "I want this for my birthday." How does a two-year-old know they get stuff for a birthday? Do they even know what a birthday is?*
- *The train your three-year-old makes out of the kitchen chairs is over ten feet long.*
- *No one has you over for dinner anymore. (Have you had a family with more than five kids over for dinner lately?)*

Seven
Chocolate Chip Cookies

IT WAS ONE of those beautiful spring Saturday afternoons with the sun shining brightly when I asked myself, "What am I doing in this hot house baking? I want to be outside!"

Then I recalled multiple teenage voices whining: "I'm hungry. Why are there no snacks to eat?" and "Is it okay if I invite a family to church tomorrow and for lunch afterward?"

Looking out our large kitchen window, I spotted the unsightly gravel flung by the snow plow onto the roadside. The new spring grass was now desperately trying to peek through. Even as the grass called out for my help, I knew feeding my "starving" children had to come first.

A short time later, my four-year-old came sauntering in. Since he lived for the neighbour boys to come over and play, I was genuinely surprised he wasn't happy playing outside with the others today.

"What ya doin', Mom?" he asked casually.

"I'm baking chocolate chip cookies!" I responded, knowing they were his all-time favourite.

"*Yes!*" he shouted with a pump of the arm, as if pulling on the air horn of a transport truck. Off he ran. A couple of minutes later,

Chocolate Chip Cookies

one of the curious neighbour boys peeped his sweet head around the kitchen door frame. With all the boldness of a seven-year-old boy, he asked, "Mrs. Schreuders? Could you let us know when the chocolate chip cookies are ready?"

"Absolutely," I replied with a grin. Then, after a quick and sincere thank you, I watched him slip back around the corner.

Ten minutes later, I was armed with six large, warm cookies on a plate. I passed the warm, gooey cookies out and poured the juice. Then, after agreeing they could take a game to play on the well-used picnic table outside, I was again approached boldly.

"Can we have another plate of cookies to take to the picnic table?"

It sure does a mother's heart good to hear that her homemade cookies are worth a second, although his following innocent statement caught me a little off guard: "When my mom bakes cookies, we're allowed to eat them all."

Shocked, I looked back at my hidden counter topped *full* with the baking I had just completed.

"Well, here in our house, we only eat one or two at a time," I returned.

With an exaggerated pout on his sweet lips, and shoulders slumped over, he slowly returned with heavy feet toward the picnic table outside. Turning back to the heaped counter, I considered if all this baking would realistically even last till Monday for lunches. On second thought, maybe I'd better bake a cake too.

Family at Large

Large Family's Chocolate Chip Cookies Recipe

Ingredients:
- *3 cups margarine*
- *3 cups white sugar*
- *1 1/2 cups brown sugar*
- *6 eggs*
- *3 tsp. baking soda*
- *9 cups flour*
- *4 cups chocolate chips*

Method:
Mix well.
Drop on greased cookie sheet.
Bake for 10-12 minutes at 350 F.

Makes A LOT!!!

Large Family Motto: If you don't have enough to share ... hide!

Eight
Surprise Vacation

BOY, WOULD I love to take my family on vacation, I thought one day. *But would a surprise vacation for a large family even be possible? Could I plan a surprise vacation for our family of eleven?*

Well, Jim and I were determined to give it our best try.

First, we decided where to go: the Wheels Inn in Chatham, for three days and two nights.

Next, I caught my oldest son, Derek, alone in the driveway one cold evening after a busy day at his full-time construction job. Thinking this might be our last vacation with the whole family present, I did my best to encourage him to join us. I told him we were planning a March Break vacation for everyone and gently, pleadingly, encouraged him to try to take time off.

"What is it?" he asked. "Will I have fun? Where are we going?"

"You must trust us. But you can't tell the others anything, since it's a surprise."

I had to secretly find caretakers for our precious pets and daily newspaper delivery. I also had to let the kids' bosses know they couldn't work those days, and all without my perceptive children finding out. Finally, in February, I had to find out if their bathing suits would still fit without arousing curiosity.

The anticipated day arrived bright, and I bubbled with eager excitement. I smiled as I watched our children sleep soundly in their beds, without knowing what the next few days held. Soon, I gently woke them, telling them that it was time to get up. Breakfast was ready.

"Why do we need to get up?"

"It's a holiday!"

"Let us sleeeeep!"

They just groaned and rolled over, but with a smile I informed them that they needed to pack their duffel bags for three days and two nights.

Suddenly, they were all wide awake and sitting upright in their rumpled beds!

"Why?"

"Where are we going?"

"But I have newspapers to deliver!"

"What about the dog? The bunny? The birds? Who will feed them?"

The concerned questions all came at once.

"It's all taken care of," I informed them before listing who would deliver the newspapers and feed the pets. I also assured them that their bosses had already been told.

"What about my fish?" piped up a small voice.

Oh right. I had forgotten the precious fish. After a quick call to a neighbour, we had the assurance that the fish would be well cared for.

Jim and I did much smiling during the loud, talkative breakfast as we deflected their questions and wild guesses about where we were going.

With a sly smirk, Derek offered to drive one of our two minivans so Jim and I could drive together. The only downfall was that we would have to tell him where we were going.

Surprise Vacation

"Nice try, Derek," I said, my smile growing even wider. "But Dad is taking the boys in the blue van, and I'm taking the girls in the red van."

After loading the minivans, Jim and I each carried a walkie talkie. Then I left with the baby and five giggling girls for some shopping, bathing suits being high on our list. The three older boys helped Jim with some odd jobs left to do around the house. Then they gradually made their way to the store to meet up with us.

"We're here!" came Jim's crackly voice over the walkie talkie. He and the three eager boys were just walking in. "Where are you?"

We gave them our exact coordinates as we tried on the last bathing suit. We then headed to the busy checkout, paid for our purchases, and filed out of the store in record time.

The next exciting stop was the coveted fast food restaurant across the street. We only sporadically went there, as the older boys needed two generous meals to fill up, making it extra expensive. But we wanted to make this weekend a special treat, and as we saw the kids' excitement, we knew we had hit the mark.

"If this is all we do, it's *great!*" Nathan exclaimed.

But by now, they all knew there was even more to come—and they were eager to find out what that "more" was.

We informed the children that we still had almost two hours of driving ahead of us. This didn't quiet their excitement, though. They were still intent on guessing our destination.

A few hours later, we pulled into the Wheels Inn parking lot. A beautiful hush fell over us.

"Are we staying here?" came the shocked question.

Not only did we rarely go out for fast food, but we *never* went to hotels!

Their anticipation rose again as I went to the main office to register our family. As I exited afterward, I could tell by Jim's tense pose that he was more than ready to get everyone settled. Standing impatiently between the two vans, he was trying to answer the kids' countless questions as they hung out of the van windows.

We then found our three attached rooms and unloaded the heavy luggage. We also brought in a cooler with milk, bread, margarine, jam, and various snacks, having decided to bring our own food to keep expenses down.

At last we went to find the nearby minigolf course. With the baby snuggled close in my arms, I watched from the sidelines as the delighted kids and Jim played.

"Mom, this is so much fun!" Derek declared for all to hear, wearing a huge smile. "And all we did so far is minigolf!"

Next, the kids made their way to the electric bumper cars. Jim offered to take the sleeping baby so I could join the kids. They turned to me, pleasantly surprised that I had quietly joined the line behind them.

"You're coming with us?" came the disbelieving smiles.

"Yes, you're not having all the fun. I want some too."

Jim and I took turns with the baby while the kids dragged us from one wild ride to another. For one brief moment, we found ourselves quietly standing in the middle of the indoor amusement park, watching. Oh, the radiant smiles, and the happy kids were grinning too! What else struck us was how our beautiful kids continued on the many rides *together*, the older ones carefully helping the younger. No one wanted the other to miss out. We were so proud of our children and how they got along. Over the next two days, our wound-up kids played games and hopped on and off various rides.

Unfortunately, the second night turned out to be a totally different story. After a fun-filled day and an enjoyable dinner at our family's favourite restaurant, everyone welcomed their temporary beds. We were fast asleep when a loud knock came from the boys' adjoining door. Derek announced in a loud whisper that Nathan was sick and throwing up. After cleaning the foul-smelling room as best we could, I tucked the reluctant boys back into their beds. Returning to my bed, I let my mind wander back to a restful place when I was rudely awakened again. This time I heard the girls' adjoining door open. Desiree loudly announced that Melissa was sick. Well, from then on, they dropped like flies.

This being our last day, we packed and loaded everything in the two vans a few hours later. Then we slowly made the long, painful drive home. Multiple stops were needed to empty the seemingly forever-full sick buckets. Everyone was grateful to finally arrive safely home to their beds. The kids still talk about how great the surprise trip was, even if it did end on a sour note.

You know you have a large family when …

- *Your family doesn't know the latest TV shows because more time is spent with others. "You really should watch more TV" was a typical response we received when discussing our lack of TV knowledge. Then, looking around at our children, they continued, "Then you wouldn't have this problem."*
- *Your idea of shopping is to run into a store looking only for the article of clothing you need and then run back out again. I first realized this when my teenage daughter (#5 in the lineup) came home from a friend's house and told me about browsing, as if it was foreign to me. She told her friend's mother, "We never do this. This is fun!"*

Nine
Mom to the Rescue!

I WAS EXHAUSTED from a long day of activities and errands in town with my younger children. While pulling into the driveway, I looked down at the lit-up gas gauge, dinging its empty signal. Hauling my purchases and small children into the house, I thought about starting dinner and getting the older children ready for youth group. I met Desiree in the kitchen, and she agreed to take her two younger brothers to youth group, as my day had already been exhausting.

By 6:30, the kids were fed and the older ones were off to youth in one of our two Grand Caravans. I cleaned up the kitchen while Jim played with the younger ones. By 7:00, we started the kids' bedtime routine of getting dressed into pjs, brushing teeth, and having story time! With little ones tucked in cozy for the night, I could finally start to wind down. Before long, the peaceful silence was pierced by the ringing of the telephone. Reluctantly, I answered it.

"Mom, I accidentally locked the keys in the car. Can you bring the spare set?" Desiree's happy-go-lucky voice came through the telephone.

"Desiree! That defeats the reason for you going to town instead of me now, doesn't it?" I couldn't help but respond with exasperation.

Mom to the Rescue!

"Yes. Sorry, Mom."

"I'm coming (sigh), but I'll have to go to Mitchell first. I need gas."

"Thanks, Mom … Sorry, Mom."

After grabbing my wallet and explaining to Jim where I was going, I jumped into the near-empty van and started for the closest gas station. The only problem with this was that I was going north instead of west. So my twenty-five-minute trip to the church would now take about forty minutes.

I finally reached the quiet gas station and filled up the empty gas tank. Then, quickly throwing my wallet on the passenger seat, I headed the van toward the church, wishing I had filled up earlier in the day when already in town.

Meanwhile, five minutes after I left for the gas station, Nathan called home.

"Hey, Dad! Can you tell Mom she doesn't need to come because we got the van unlocked? Nico got it opened with a coat hanger."

"Uummm, Mom is already on her way. She will not be happy. You better put the keys back in the van and lock the doors," Jim instructed. So being the obedient children they are … they did!

Arriving at the church, I noticed only a few youths left, waiting with my kids until I arrived. So I swung my van alongside the locked one and jumped out. Then, after unlocking their doors, I hopped back into my vehicle.

"Thanks, Mom!" came a call from a group of giggling girls in front of the now-unlocked van.

"I'm going home with Mom!" my son Nathan yelled to his sister as he jumped in the passenger seat beside me and slammed the door.

Upon reaching home, I let out a huge sigh and heard my bed calling for me. Just before opening the van door, I reached down to grab my small wallet from between the two front seats.

My wallet was not there.

I looked at the seat where Nathan had sat earlier. Not there either. Getting out of the van, I walked around to the passenger side, looking at the ground outside, on the van floor, around the front seat, and even under it. The wallet was nowhere to be found. Now, as my grandmother used to say in Dutch, "Je maakt mij zo kokend! (You make me so boiling!)." I marched into the house to ask Nathan if he had seen my wallet when he jumped into the van.

"No, Mom," he replied.

Jim even came out to help me look for it, but I was over-tired and in tears by then. As the other kids drove up, we asked if they had seen my little black wallet in the church parking lot before they left. Of course, they had not seen the wallet, but that didn't mean it wasn't there. So Jim drove the twenty-five minutes with his loony-bin wife back to the church.

I held my breath as we approached the dark church. We could see the one street light glowing down onto the parking lot. Coming over the hill, in the middle of the parking lot, lay my wallet for the world to see. Then, with a huge sigh, I released the pent-up air I had kept inside. We retrieved my wallet from its airy location and made the twenty-five-minute trek back home, exhausted.

It wasn't until a few months later that the rest of the story accidentally came out, and even I had to laugh.

You know you have a large family when ...

- *You realize that the money you could have saved had you only gotten your driving instructor's certificate BEFORE the first student driver.*
- *You have more than one of your vehicles in the hospital emergency parking lot at a time. Sitting in the hospital emergency department with your youngest, you hear a familiar voice. Looking out in the hall, you see your oldest guiding the fourth child, holding rags on his cut and bleeding hand.*
- *You go to the hospital emergency department, they ask you if your child has allergies, and you can't remember which child has what allergy.*
- *Your youngest son says to your oldest son, "MY mom says we can't do that!"*

Ten
Finding God

> *"As the deer pants for streams of water,
> so my soul pants for you, my God. My soul thirsts for God,
> for the living God. When can I go and meet with God?"*
> (Psalm 42:1–2)

I WAS LOOKING for quiet—quiet to find myself, my core ... God. But first, I needed to put things into proper perspective. "I want out!" was too broad a term. To narrow it down, I needed to step into a padded room where I heard nothing but the Lord. Yes, I wanted to spend time with Jim, just the two of us, but I must find God back first. I wanted to hear Him. I wanted to know what I was going to do and how to do it.

Here I was again, crying. Was I self-centred? Was it wrong to want some "me" time? A time when I could sit and reflect? A time to be silent and hear God? Oh, what I wouldn't give to hear the Lord's voice! Or to even listen for Him. For now, I sat wistfully in my room, with kids' voices yelling through the registers as they use them as telephones, and children holding conversations outside my bedroom door. My toddler was screaming upstairs. People might say I was "alone" in my room, but I didn't feel alone.

I tried earlier to get away. I went into our laundry room, figuring I would fold laundry. It had to be quiet there, with the washer and dryer humming their songs. So there I stood, laundry baskets all around my feet. The shelf to my right was broken. The top shelf was precariously hanging on, and the middle shelf was missing its contents, which were scattered around the floor. I hoped the two little boys wouldn't come here because they could get seriously hurt. I knew I'd done two or three loads of laundry that needed folding in this jungle of baskets, but which ones were they? Nathan's clothes basket looked like one of those baskets, but I had other things to do. Boy, did I ever have so much to do (sigh)!

"I'm bored!" said one of the older children.

To which I replied, "Well, help me clean."

"No thanks," was the quick response.

"You won't let us play computer, and there are no dogs to walk," whimpered Christina, on her bed in tears.

Why couldn't we work together? Was it even possible? Could I find something for us all to do together? Then, in return, they would help me on their own ... maybe?

I had to clean the house. Sunday, with its usual company, was rapidly approaching. Since these guests were newcomers, the house would probably be toured. Who would help clean it?

"Why, Mom? This is the way we live!"

This was NOT the way I wanted to live. Order was much better than chaos!

Someone yelled, "Dad's home, and he has Mom's new shelf!"

Oh, maybe one of my prayers had been answered. Either that or the nagging wife got what she wanted just to shut her up. Was that guilt I was feeling? Lord, where are you in all this?

I wrote this when my older kids lived at home and we only had two vehicles in the driveway. Those were the days when the children seemed to be *everywhere*! Reading back, I could almost feel that desperate time in my life. Have you ever felt that way—

overwhelmed, alone, desperate? Last year, I happened upon a book called *Desperate—Hope for the Mom Who Needs to Breathe*[1] by Sarah Mae and Sally Clarkson. I cried for the first three chapters, realizing that had been me. Finally, someone who understood what I was going through all those years ago.

I wish I had known then what I know now. I wish I'd had mentors! Of course, I had friends, but I wished I had found a good, seasoned homeschool mom to talk to. Someone older, someone who knew what I was going through and had the same ideals as I did. Thinking back, I realize that homeschooling was starting to catch on when we started. Would there have been such a person? Someone who went to the Bible for answers to my questions and had encouraging words to help me through those hard days? Someone who would pray with me? Was there such a mentor out there for me? Knowing what I know now, could I ever be such a mentor for someone else?

I encourage all you moms out there to find someone older and faithful in their walk with the Lord. Someone who will continuously encourage you to look up to our calming, peaceful Lord and the goal of heaven. Someone who would encourage you to focus on something other than daily chaos and happenings around us. As I tried to look to God daily, I realized how much of life is out of my hands and in His. Things don't happen because of anything I do, even though He might use me. I don't accomplish anything in my own strength. It's God's plan, His perfect plan. How could I have ever thought any different? Yes, some days I look back and realize I had tried to do it my way. On other days I don't see it until much later. I had even laughed out loud on those days when I looked and saw how the Lord physically moved me out of the way so He could work in my and His children's lives.

I have done everything possible to raise my kids to know the Lord. I believe with all my heart that my dear children know who

---

[1] Sarah Mae, *Desperate*. (Tennessee: Thomas Nelson, 2013)

the Lord is. But as they get older, I have to stand back more and more and let them take what they've been taught and make it their own. Some of my kids are fighting against that. Others follow the Christian life out of tradition because it's what they know. Then there are those who are seeking out the Lord with their whole heart.

All my children will face opposition from the devil, no matter where they are in life. Jim and I pray for all of them every day! We beg and plead with the Lord Almighty to put people in their path to guide them to a closer walk with Him. Our goal is not to raise intelligent, friendly, or well-behaved kids (even if that was my original goal). Those goals have moved to second place. Now my goal is to raise kids who will be with us in heaven someday!

God has promised many things to me, including hope and a great future (1 Peter 1:3–12). Those promises will always stand no matter what happens in my life or my kids' lives. Every day I put our future in God's hands. Sometimes it's hard watching those difficult days unfold; some answers to prayer don't seem to happen quickly enough, and others don't happen the way I want to see them. But each day, God is working inside my children and me, making us into the people He wants us to be and teaching us lessons He wants us to learn. Now the most important thing about my—our—future is following Him. Because, in the end, it's all about finding God. He is the reason we are here in the first place.

Family at Large

You know you have a large family when ...

- *Each laundry load is a specific colour, such as red, yellow, or maybe green.*
- *The laundry line is full of jeans.*
- *The laundry line is full every day.*
- *You get a nice suntan from the time you spend hanging out laundry.*
- *The laundry room, which is close to a large bathroom, makes an ideal "family closet." This sure has kept the amount of laundry down in other locations of the house.*
- *The person behind the counter at Mac's Milk is shocked when you tell them you have eight jugs of milk to purchase and proceeds to ask if your family members are milkaholics. One day I bought only seven jugs of milk. "Did someone move out?" the cashier asked me. A huge smile spread over my face as I answered, "Yes, actually, my oldest just moved out last week."*

Eleven
Always Expect the Unexpected

HAVING TEN KIDS in the family means you can never "plan" your days. A general goal, maybe, but never a set plan. One Saturday in September, my son Nico, eighteen years old, asked if having his new friend over for lunch after church was okay. That was okay with us, as we always love meeting our kids' new friends. We tried to do special little things every now and then for each child. So that day, I decided to put spaghetti on tomorrow's menu, since it was one of Nico's favourites. Having four cans of sauce in my hand instead of the usual three, I decided the little extra could go into Nico's lunch next week. So I set those four cans on the clean counter next to the plugged-in crock pot, where a two-pound package of spiced hamburger simmered.

Sunday morning came, and I readied myself for church. I drained and crumbled the cooked hamburger, adding the four cans of sauce to the crock pot. I turned from the counter, where I'd placed a large package of noodles beside the simmering meat sauce. I was thankful for our sizeable, handmade pine dining room table, which comfortably seats twelve. When Jim and I had made this table a few years back, we'd made sure an additional chair could be added to each end easily, making it big enough for fourteen.

I joined my family as we ate our "Sunday cereal," also known as "Lucky Charms." This treat was only found on our table Sunday mornings. While we ate a leisurely breakfast, I overheard my twenty-year-old daughter, Desiree, mention to her four younger sisters that two of her friends were coming over today. My mind raced back to the week before. When she asked if anything special was happening next Sunday, so that she could have these two friends over, whom she had not seen in a while. I told her nothing special was happening, and the girls were more than welcome to come. I leaned over and whispered to Jim this added information in case he hadn't heard. As breakfast came to a close, everyone sped up. The kids were trying to use the only two bathrooms we had to prepare for church.

It was 8:45 and time to *start* leaving the house. I did a last-minute check on the kids. Do all the girls have their hair done? I could see it in their eyes. How does Mom know when we don't comb our long, blonde hair? But I *know*! Okay, on the hair. Check. Do the little ones all have their shirts tucked in and good socks on, not the Sunday "holey" ones? Check.

"Everyone, shoes on and out the door!" commanded Jim.

The older ones helped the younger ones slip into their shoes, and they all made their way to the three waiting vehicles we'd be taking to church today. Jim directed traffic into the vehicles while I grabbed the church library books and our three-year-old's mini backpack in case of a potty emergency.

Sitting in church, taking up a whole pew, I looked over to see Jim smiling from ear to ear, just as I was. We love having a full house *and* a full bench. As the church service concluded, Nathan, our seventeen-year-old, came over to inform me that he couldn't drive his little brother Calvin back home and asked if we had room.

"Okay, but what about Desiree? How is she going to get home?" I questioned him, only to receive an "I-don't-know" shrug.

So I then hunted down Desiree and her two friends. After I explained the situation, her friends offered to take her to our house when they came for lunch. With that settled, I made my way through the crowd and herded our two little boys quickly to the door. As I walked out into the sunshine, I firmly held the two boys back as Nathan passed us with his "new" standard pickup truck—a Ford Ranger. You know, those little pickup trucks a six-foot-tall son had to "put on" to drive? Well, he had two of his approximately six-foot-tall friends with him. The boys had the windows down with their arms out to give each other more shoulder room. I didn't know how they shifted the gears, but I guess a mother doesn't need to know some things. I continued to my van with the two little boys in tow and mentally tallied up two more for lunch.

"I think I'll have to run to the garden when I get home to pick lettuce to make a salad," I said to no one in particular.

Once home, I put a huge pot of water on the stove for the spaghetti noodles. I remembered having a large bag of buns in the freezer, so I quickly took them out, put them on a tray, and set them to warm in the oven while I went to the garden for fresh lettuce. Walking through the house to the door, I passed people here and there. Some were waiting in line by the bathroom to change their clothes, others were playing games at the table, and others were talking and hanging out. Finally, in the mudroom, I slipped on my shoes and headed out the door to the garden.

I picked a hearty bunch of fresh lettuce and returned to the busy house. On my way, a white car pulled into the driveway. Approaching the car, I saw Derek, who lived down the road about five minutes. We usually only saw him on Tuesday nights when he came for a family dinner and to tell us how his week had gone. So this visit was an unexpected yet pleasant surprise. Chatting with him for only a minute, I directed him to Jim, who was on the other side of the house, before returning to the kitchen to prepare the Caesar salad.

"Hey! Look who's here!" I heard Jim's happy voice through the open kitchen window in front of me as he greeted Derek.

Another one for dinner. Will I have enough to feed them? I hollered through the window for Jim to please bring in more lettuce for a bigger salad.

The buns were almost finished toasting in the oven as the seventeen people found their seats. We were ready to begin our buffet-style meal. Jim asked for a blessing on the food while I again silently asked the Lord for enough food. "Jesus feeds the five thousand" entered my head, and I relaxed. All seventeen people dug into the spaghetti lunch the Lord had provided, with many taking seconds. Jim laughed as our oldest heaped his plate.

"Good to have you for lunch, Derek!" Jim and I tried to listen to two, three, four, or more conversations around us. Everyone seemed to be enjoying themselves. I looked at Nico's friend and wondered what she thought of all this. What do our kids tell their friends to prepare them for … for this?

Once everyone confirmed they had plenty to eat, we finished by listening to God's Word and saying a prayer of thanks for the food He provided. I silently thanked Him for enough food.

"Cleanup should go fast with all the extra help to do the dishes," Jim announced with a smile.

The topic was again about how the dishwasher had not worked for five years. Or was it six years now? But once again, it being Sunday, Jim offered to clean up with me. Everyone helped clean off the large table. Some joined in a competitive board game or card game. Others went for a leisurely walk on the trail by the river or on an adventurous canoe ride. Some chose to find a quiet place to read a book, and the little ones played with their toys.

It wasn't long before we were left alone to do the dishes. I leaned against Jim from behind, giving him a big hug, and whispered, "You loved this, didn't you?"

"Yes, I did! I love it when the house is full!" he responded, grinning from ear to ear, his hands deep in the sudsy dishwater.

I squeezed him and stepped over to the dirty stove to check on the empty pots. As I peered over the edge, I was pleasantly surprised to see that the pots were *not* empty at all.

"Two baskets of fish left over. The Lord has provided once again," I whispered, smiling.

Then I silently gave God another prayer of thanksgiving. Even though the unexpected happens day by day, God is there to work it all out. Thank you, Lord!

You know you have a large family when ...
- *Your husband encourages you to push that newborn baby out because he has only half an hour before he must be at a piano recital for two older kids.*
- *Your two-and-a-half-year-old introduces himself to his twenty-year-old brother when he comes home for our scheduled Tuesday night dinner. "Hi! I'm Joshie!"*
- *When there are multiple names on the inside pant pocket listing all the previous owners, all of whom are from your own household.*

Twelve
Lifestyle

QUIETLY SITTING AT my laptop in the dining room one afternoon, I intently worked, preparing school lessons. Melissa approached with a short question. Wanting to finish what I was doing before answering, I confess, I ignored her.

"You never let us!" came the snarky whine as she stomped off. Okay, she had my attention now.

"Wait! Get back here," I called after her.

"But you never let us," she persisted.

"Never let you what?" I questioned, at a loss as to what our conversation was about.

"You never let us watch TV!"

"When did I say you couldn't?" I was still baffled.

"You just shook your head no," she informed me.

"No, I didn't." I realized my voice was also going up into a whine.

"Yes, you did!" she stated.

I wasn't going to argue, so I returned the conversation back to the original question.

This slowly became an ongoing dilemma in our house, to the point where the kids reworded their questions as negative to get

Lifestyle

what they wanted. When I shook my head no, they would say, "Thanks!" and run off.

One day Jim mentioned that my head would shake from left to right as if I was saying no, whenever I was concentrating on something. So off to the doctor I went, and after explaining the situation, she sent me to a specialist.

"It says here in your chart you have narcolepsy?" the specialist questioned after quick introductions.

"Narcolepsy? I'm sorry, I don't know what that is," I replied.

"It's when you suddenly fall asleep at any given time," he answered.

"I don't have that!" I declared. "I have medication to help me stay awake while driving long distances, though."

Looking at me with disbelief, he began some tests, pointing out that my head tilted slightly to the left. He wasn't concerned about this, as it was probably a result of the tumour removal surgery I'd had ten years earlier.

"I don't see too much shaking, although it is there. I can give you a little Botox in your neck to settle it, though, if you'd like," he explained.

Botox? I was shocked!

"No, I think I'll leave it," I replied after a short hesitation.

"That's fine," he stated. "I'll see you in about ten years, as it will gradually worsen."

Not believing what I was hearing, I sat stunned. Finally, after the uncomfortable, quick, and seemingly abrupt visit, I watched him leave the room.

A week later, I was talking to my friendly family doctor about the narcolepsy on my record.

"I don't understand how that got on my record!"

"You mean to tell me you've never been tested for this?" she questioned.

"Never," I said, trying to keep my voice calm.

"Okay. How about this? I book you for a sleep test so we can rule out narcolepsy," she advised.

"Yes, please!"

I was very thankful when the day finally arrived that I was able to talk to yet another doctor, one with more personality, about the upcoming sleep test.

After getting over the shock of my ten kids, he asked, "How many hours of sleep did you get before you had kids?"

I was stumped.

"That was about twenty-three years ago! I don't know!"

"Guess," he encouraged with a smile.

"I guess I'd go to bed at ten and be up at about eight," I guesstimated.

"So about ten hours. How many do you think you get now?" he asked.

"I'd be lucky to get to bed by eleven or twelve by the time the kids are all settled in for the night, and I'm up at five when others have to go to work," I answered. "So about five or six hours."

Writing this on his chart, he explained how the sleep test works.

Jim drove me to the sleep clinic late one afternoon. We agreed on a meeting place and time after the sleep test, as I would have a few hours before he could pick me up after work. After he picked me up, we planned to have a dinner date.

I was connected to all kinds of wires at the clinic and then tucked in for the night at 9:00 PM. Sleeping and being awakened regularly was annoying, but as the night went into the day and I was forced to nap, I quickly got over it.

Feeling well-rested by the time I was free of the wires, I joked with the nurse, "Can I come back next week? I was enjoying the vacation."

After a few weeks, I met with the amusing sleep test doctor.

Lifestyle

"According to the test, you do not have a medical condition," he stated, pausing to let the news sink in. "You have a lifestyle condition."

"All this just to find out having ten kids makes me tired?" I asked in disbelief.

With a smile, he added, "Once your youngest child is grown and you can get a good night's sleep, you shouldn't have a problem anymore."

"He's four! That will be a while. What do I do till then?" I asked.

"Well, the sleep test shows you need five to ten-minute naps to overcome your tiredness. Once you start to wake up, get up. Don't linger; it will make it worse." He then asked if I'd had trouble driving to this appointment.

"Yes," I replied.

"Did you take kids with you?" he questioned.

"No."

"Before you leave, try having a short nap. See if that helps."

I thanked him for his valuable time and positive test results. Then proceeding out to the parking lot, I quietly sat in my van, letting it all sink in. After a few moments, I listened to the doctor's advice and napped for five minutes. Surprisingly, I drove home for one and a half hours with no problem. From then on, I gave myself afternoon naps for ten to fifteen minutes, which I took while the kids washed the lunch dishes and wouldn't miss me. I felt more alert now, and my tired brain was less foggy. Thankfully no medication was required for this lifestyle condition!

Family at Large

You know you have a large family when ...

- *Taking a "few" kids to town means three or four.*
- *Your youngest says, "There isn't going to be any more names left when I have kids!"*
- *A family rate doesn't apply to your family. "Sorry, sir, a family is only two adults and two kids!" We soon learned to read the fine print before showing up.*
- *The high school teachers tell your kids to put on their resume that they come from a large family because it shows that they can work well with others.*
- *You find a location that has soccer for all your kids on the same night so that you can go from one soccer game to the next, but never watch an entire game.*
- *You're oblivious to the fact that your child's immunizations are six or seven years past due.*

Thirteen
What about Me?

HERE I AM, a unique mom for almost twenty-three years now, but I admit it has taken me this long to understand, really understand, my amazing role in this world.

I remember when I had four small, blonde-haired, blue-eyed children. I dare say that was the busiest time in my entire life. Now, with older kids, I could direct traffic, assign jobs, and keep moving. Back then, I did it all. I changed dirty diapers, handed out boring snacks, did mountains of laundry, cleaned house, did grimy dishes, did more laundry, gardened, entertained, and was even the capable fix-it person. That was all me. I would practically follow my untidy kids around, cleaning up after them between laundry loads. Back then, spending quality time with my kids was not my focal point, so when my loving husband suggested we home-school, my jaw dropped. Didn't I do enough already? I was an organized person, a neat freak, you might say. I have been told it was because I had something to prove while growing up. That made sense to me now but not to my four little kids, who wanted a good-natured mom to play with them. As I was growing up, between the ages of ten and fourteen, my mom was very ill. Being the oldest of three, I was responsible for cooking, cleaning, laundry, shopping, and other household chores. I believe God prepared me to run a household efficiently during these younger years. Meanwhile, I have always felt like I didn't know how to play.

Once, I remember reading a juvenile library book to the kids about a carefree mother and a playful son. They imagined being in different places doing extraordinary things *while* she still did her daily chores. This clever idea seemed so much fun and came naturally to her. I wondered if I could be like that. How could I incorporate imagination into my everyday chores? I didn't feel like I was cut out for this extensive vocation. What was our amazing God doing by giving me all these impressionable children? Surely someone else would be more suitable than me. At that time in my life, I wanted to be anywhere but home. My temper was short because I believed I was supposed to be doing something more significant with my dry life. I feared missing out on what God wanted me to do; great things and awe-inspiring opportunities were passing me by, or so I thought. And I was right! Great things were passing me by—my precious kids. They were growing up right before me, and I wasn't there for them.

Physically I cared for them: bandaging cuts, making meals, and clothing them. But I wasn't there for them emotionally or, more importantly, spiritually most days. Instead, grudgingly, I seemed to be rushing us right through life.

Let's get this done so we can get on to bigger and better things! ran my train of thought. Oh, how that brings stinging tears to my eyes now. But at that time, I wanted more for *me*!

Now, six kids later, I see more clearly. This *is* my job, the big and glorious thing God has always planned for me, his precious daughter, to do. *This* was the most fulfilling job in the world. Because I realized this, my kids now had me, all of me, all ten of them. I was their devoted mother, the only one they would know (except for a future spouse) who loved them with all her heart, soul, mind, and strength. I would do my best to care for their physical, mental, and spiritual needs, for they were the only precious riches I could take into heaven. So I would treat them with respect, love them unconditionally, and guide them through life to that goal—heaven!

I tried to concentrate on sitting still and watching my younger children play, as I could see now how time was racing past, like the Indy 500. I found myself discovering ways to spend quality time with these precious gifts from God. It seemed like just yesterday that I became a new mom. Now I blink to find each of my children has grown into a handsome man or beautiful woman. It's as if I just turned and all that late-night rocking magically turned to late-night talking. Now their searching souls, rather than their soft skin, need soothing. Even though we all keep moving, seemingly in opposite directions, love keeps us together like an umbilical cord that had never been cut. Strange how you could be in your own skin yet feel another soul struggle so hard. My family is a part of me. When one of my children doesn't visit or call, I feel like I'm missing a significant piece of me. When someone struggles, I struggle with how to help them. When one talks back, a mind-boggling fear comes over me: "What have I done wrong in raising this child?" It's like watching your heart carelessly walking around outside of your body. Maybe I, as a mom, will always live with a bit of each of my children's cherished hearts in my inner walls.

Now I look back at the small, insignificant things and realize that they were the huge, vital things. To me, they were drudgery, and I struggled to get through them. Now I see that all those moments amounted to life—their lives and mine—a big thing. Now I can say with John, "*I have no greater joy than to hear that my children are walking in the truth*" (3 John 4).

Family at Large

You know you have a large family when ...

- *You take the time to watch the antics of your younger ones because you know the time flew with the older ones.*
- *You look at your newborn baby and think you've seen them somewhere before.*
- *The driveway shows signs of company—all the time.*
- *Vehicles were once on the side of the road in the evenings because there wasn't any room in the driveway after everyone returned home from work. When we put in a second driveway, and there still was not enough room.*
- *You draw a diagram on the chalkboard to figure out who goes in which vehicle in order to get to church.*
- *You move as close to the wall as possible when the phone rings because of the stampede of children trying to answer it first.*

Fourteen
Camping

CAMPING IS A tremendous thing when you have a sizable family. Just to clarify, we probably don't do your kind of camping; we don't do trailers, motor homes, or cottages. We call our camping real camping, with multiple tents! I'm definitely not one for camping in the rain but am rather a fair-weather camper. So when we go camping, I'm known for taking an enormous tarp, the biggest one I can find. This oversized blue tarp is comparable to a security blanket—my security blanket. If there's any chance of rain, that huge tarp is strung up before we even think of setting up any tents. One year as I struggled with this tarp, I looked over and saw my husband and dad—side by side—shaking their heads at me in unison. On the other hand, my kids and husband *love* camping, so a mother has to do what a mother has to do ... *camp*!

The best way to make camping happen is to make it easy, or in other words (my words), get organized! I began by collecting a second set of durable dishes. When my grandmothers moved into senior homes, I asked for some of their silverware, pots, and pans. I bought melamine plates, bowls, and tin cups from the local dollar store. (I needed the durable type of dishes so that they wouldn't break when jostled around on the way to and from camping.

Camping supplies seemed to take a beating during the rough ride in the blue trailer towed behind one of our vans, or packed in the back of one of the pickup trucks we've had over the years.) I found a broken Rubbermaid three-drawer set. Garbage in someone's mind, but something I fixed up to work as a two-drawer set. I placed all the plates, bowls, and cups in the top drawer, and the silverware, tablecloths, large utensils, coffee/tea, sugar, and Bible in the bottom drawer.

In a bright green tote, I placed the deflated air mattresses, extra plugs, a mattress repair kit, and the small yellow air pump that connects to my vehicle's cigarette lighter. A large clear tote with a white lid held the collapsible water bag, the kettle nestled inside a large pan, and a second, slightly smaller pan in the black-bottomed frying pan.

A second large, flat clear tote resembled a junk drawer, holding anything else we might need—things such as a slightly dull hatchet, sharp camping knife, old hammer, and even a rusty wrench that was needed to connect the ancient camp stove (handed down from my grandfather) to the full propane tank. That all-important monkey wrench was also used to assist Jim in holding the metal cooking rack to the fire pit rack so that all our dinners didn't fall into the open fire. Over the years, Jim had taught my children and me that it was authentic camping only if at least one piece of dinner meat fell into that open flame. This "junk" tote also contained a small bottle of dish soap, a reused mustard bottle containing laundry detergent, an old red Tupperware lunch box with clothespins, a nest of blue clothesline, red nylon twine, and the all-essential coloured duct tape. If those rainy days occurred, I was equipped with a few dog-eared card games, colouring books with missing pages, used crayons, and well-read *Reader's Digests*, which I recycled at a thrift shop every few years. We couldn't forget the sand-covered suntan lotion, bug spray, multiple mini flashlights, a Ziplock baggie of extra batteries, multiple folded garbage bags, and a crushed roll of paper towels. This tote also contained a large broom minus its handle, which was used to sweep out the sandy tents. (My beach-loving family thoroughly enjoyed camping where there was *lots* of sand. It wouldn't be successful camping unless sand was brought absentmindedly into my large tent or my shared double sleeping bag. Yuk!)

My son's girlfriend, Jessica, came camping with us one year. I heard her whisper to my son Nathan that she couldn't believe how everything was so organized.

"You could tell my mom we were going camping, and she could have the van packed in half an hour, except for the grocery shopping," he responded.

You see, all those stocked totes of camping gear, bagged tents, sleeping bags, and camp stoves all sat together in a corner in my crowded storage room. When it was time to go camping, we carried them out and strategically loaded the van, trailer, or pickup. I kept a miscellaneous list that had a few things in other places on our property—things such as lawn chairs, towels, sand toys, shovels, rakes, wiener sticks, wire cooking rack, card table, and a spare propane tank. Part of the list reflected our adventurous side: canoe, paddles, life jackets, and bikes with helmets. But all in all, packing for camping didn't take long.

When we brought small children, we also took along a little teepee tent Desiree made one year with her Oma. This little tent, made from PVC pipe and colourful polyester material, was used as a changing room or to give shade to the baby while we were on the hot beach. Back at the campsite, we would place a little portable potty in it, making a great little outhouse for the little ones.

An adventurous bike ride as a family, with maybe a leisure hike while we stopped here or there for good measure, was reserved for our camp mornings. We then grabbed a quick lunch and went to the sunny beach for the afternoon. People have been known to turn their curious heads when we arrived at the beach with our large family carrying large shovels and pails. The shovels—spades actually—were used to build huge piles of sand with a massive mote around them. Since we lived across the road from a small corner store that sold Chapman's ice cream, we ended up with some of their large pails. These assisted in making some fantastic sand castles.

While at the beach, we would sun ourselves, play with floaties in the water, or, better yet, get "neckie" rides from Dad or another older sibling. Meanwhile, I sat on the beach, where I attempted to read a book but often spent most of the time carefully watching and deliberately counting the kids from under my multicoloured beach umbrella. I also took the kids' pictures and handed out non-nutritional snacks! Okay, I confess I did go in the nippy water to cool off occasionally, usually after much coaxing from my frolicking kids or playful husband.

We headed back to our cozy campsite late in the afternoon to start an open fire for supper. Jim did most of the supper cooking, whether it be the tantalizing pork chops, chicken, sausages, or the typical burger and dogs! We also had a side of chips or homemade salads I'd made before coming and some cut-up veggies. After a delicious dinner, we cleaned the dirty dishes in our smaller tote. Next, we used the same tote with clean water to wash up the small, sandy kids and get them dressed for bed. Finally, the small fire was stoked again, and the marshmallows and special-to-camping munchies emerged.

The worst thing for me about camping was coming home! As the kids gradually took down the hopefully dry tents, I tried to save time by ensuring the dishes were washed well at the campsite before leaving. Then, when we arrived home, if things were dry, everything could be thrown back where it belonged, whether in the storage room or outside in the garage or shed. The only thing that remained was the laundry; let me tell you, there were mountains of it! Every year I wanted to spend the money and go to the local laundry mat, paste a large sign on the door that said, "Closed, Private Party!" and do all that smelly, sandy, wet laundry in one shot! Think about it: in a couple of hours, you could turn that mountain of dirty clothes into a sea of clean laundry.

After twenty-five years of camping, even with its challenges, I must admit that it's getting better. I'm actually enjoying myself now. So now I can take a deep breath, thank the Lord for good memories on yet another fantastic camping adventure, wonder what I was apprehensive about, and prepare for the next one … secretly thankful it's not for another couple of weeks!

You know you have a large family when …

- *Making beds is a workout all its own.*
- *In a room with two sets of bunk beds, a projectile vomiter on a top bunk gets four sets of sheets dirty.*
- *Your six-year-old can climb into your kitchen cupboard after you have taken out the large mixer and your oversized bucket of flour for baking. Then he asks if that can be his quiet place because he is mad!*
- *Your family goes on a bike ride and Dad is in front with the bike trailer, followed by multiple bikes ranging in size, ending with Mom and the smallest biker. People on the street stand, sometimes with coffee in hand, watching as if it's a parade.*

Fifteen
Date Night

WALKING ... ALONE ... TOGETHER ... finally.

Jim's two-week vacation was coming to a close, while my homeschooling would begin again the next day. This was the last day we could leave our rambunctious kids and spend some quiet time together, just Jim and I. Did we get to do this often? No, but we were doing it more than we used to do now that we had a few "built-in" babysitters. We didn't realize how much we needed this until someone recently challenged us.

"Once a week, date night! Jim, you pick the night," our friend challenged.

This sent my head reeling. Did Jim have any idea of our family's weekly schedule? Did he pay any attention to anything that I say? I could see panic as I looked into Jim's eyes—or was that a reflection of my own?

Jim thought and cautiously, very cautiously, asked, "Monday?"

Monday night—date night? My brain went through the Rolodex of weekly activities, stopping suddenly on Mondays. Bible study with the neighbourhood ladies was Monday night. But a date night—with my husband—every week? The spinning slowed, and the fog started to clear. I could change Bible study or join

Date Night

another group. With hope springing anew in my heart, I answered, "Mondays are good." I saw a smile spread across Jim's face, and he visibly relaxed. "Really good!" I added.

I must admit that the first few date nights were not peaceful or relaxing. Far from it, actually. I had a list! Yes, I am a woman of lists. I wanted to talk about this, this, *and* this. I needed answers to this, that, and the next thing. Finally, Jim clued me in.

"This date night is supposed to be a relaxing time to spend with each other. I don't want to talk about anything or make any decisions or plans. I just want to spend time with you," he stated.

Well, I felt heartbroken and touched at the same time. Realizing I probably just ruined date nights, I began pouting. I consoled myself by reasoning that date night wouldn't last anyway, right? After mulling it over, I realized how much we needed our time alone, so I decided to fight for it.

The fight paid off. I learned to relax, letting the conversation flow where it may, and you know what? God gave us the opportunities we needed to discuss those important things, and I slowly received the answers to my countless questions in God's time, not mine. As a result, date night had become a time for us to pray, talk about each of our kids, discuss what we believed and how to raise our kids, plan things, debate what our kids had been planning, or just be silent. The silence was golden! Oh, the peace that came with silence. It could renew a heart and re-energize the tired, foggy brain.

Almost four months have now passed, and I am excited to tell you that we have only missed two date nights. I never realized that Jim wanted it (and needed it) as much as I did. Today I can comfortably relax on our weekly date nights while enjoying the feel of Jim's strong hand in mine, his blue eyes watching me, making me blush like a schoolgirl all over again. That "I'm in love" feeling is back.

"Have I ever told you I love you?" he asked with raised eyebrows.

"Not lately," I flirted a little.

"Well, I love you," he said sweetly.

I couldn't help myself; I rushed into his arms and held him close, never wanting to let go, never wanting to share him with ten kids, wanting him all to myself—even if it was only for Monday date night.

Four years since we started our date nights, and after twenty-five years of marriage, even our observant kids notice when we miss one of our treasured Monday evenings. With date night, we are more on the ball in figuring out the details of our family schedule. Answers to their questions come faster. Questions that can't wait until the next date night are now written on a sticky note and placed randomly on the mirror of Mom and Dad's headboard. These questions are usually discussed before going to sleep. More importantly, the kids have noticed that we are happier parents. What kid wouldn't want that?

"Isn't it date night tonight? Why are you still here?" is what we hear on those Monday nights when we're feeling drained and dragging our feet. Of course, we usually make it a shorter date on those fatigued evenings, but we never regret having gone.

Our oldest daughter had gotten married in the past year. She told us she would do date nights too, because of the difference she had seen in us. We strongly suggest date nights to all couples!

I feel I must clarify what a real date night is. It's a night away with no interrupting kids. It's a time to talk without a younger eavesdropping ear close by. It is not a movie night or a much-needed time to go visiting with long-lost or not-so-lost friends. Those are saved for separate nights. Instead, date nights are a time to strengthen your bond with each other. This past year we've been working through a book called *The 50 Fridays Marriage Challenge* by Jeff and Lora Helton.[2] The book asks one question a week,

---

[2] Jeff Helton and Lora Helton, *The 50 Fridays Marriage Challenge: One Question a Week* (Tennessee: Howard Books, 2013).

which we read on the drive to our destination, and it helps us start an enjoyable evening of conversation. On many date nights, we select a nice walking trail in one of the small towns around our house. We find this gives us a relaxing atmosphere while helping us get some well-needed exercise together. Other nights, when the weather is not cooperating, we quietly sit in a restaurant and enjoy each other's company. Date nights are now essential to our busy lives, making time for each other when time seems nonexistent in our large family.

While reading through a couple's devotional book on date night after twenty-eight years of marriage …

Joanne: "What is something you love about your spouse that you didn't know about him or her when you first got married?"

Jim was deep in thought for many moments before his face lit up, his right hand flew up, and he pointed to heaven: "That she would have ten kids!"

Sixteen
Unpredictable Bunnies

MANY MOONS AGO, before having any kids, I helped several crafty ladies make cute fabric bunnies to sell at the local Christian school bazaar. Soft and cuddly, these bunnies were made of white flannel and stuffed with fluffy batting. We then sewed black-button eyes on each bunny, and a cute bunny nose and smile were embroidered underneath them. We then outfitted these darlings with pretty dresses, matching bonnets, and the most adorable bloomers.

A few years later, Jim fashioned a mini-church pew for the two Opa and Oma bunny rabbits I had made as a Christmas gift for my parents. My mom loved them and set them, prim and proper, in front of the fireplace in their living room.

Wanting to get them something special and unique for their thirty-fifth wedding anniversary, I thought it would be fun to make a slightly smaller bunny to represent each of their grandchildren. So I got busy making the required seven bunnies: five boy bunnies in handsome overalls and two girl bunnies in frilly dresses with matching bloomers. I made sure each child's name was placed in the corresponding bunny's left floppy ear before the special day finally arrived. Dad and Mom opened the long rectangular flower box to find seven fully dressed bunnies looking quietly up at them.

Unpredictable Bunnies

Mom fell in love instantly. They were placed around the larger Opa and Oma "Bummy Rabbits" (as the grandkids renamed them), which sat prim and proper on the mini church pew.

Soon we were expecting another precious gift from God, and I placed myself in front of the Singer sewing machine, making it hum once again. Out came another bunny, but this one would stay naked for now, as we didn't know yet if we would need a dress with bloomers or handsome overalls. We boxed the naked bunny in tissue paper, and Jim took it to work the next day, shipping it by Purolator to my unsuspecting Mom. Meanwhile, I sat at home waiting. How could a package cause so many butterflies? Finally, the phone rang. Answering it, I wondered if it would be my mom.

"Really? Is this for real?" my mom's shocked voice came through the phone.

"Yes!" I answered with a smile. "When did you get it?"

"Just now! The Purolator guy is still in the driveway!" she chuckled.

This is fun, I thought as I smiled. After this precious daughter arrived, I made the frilly dress and fancy bloomers and carefully wrote her name in the floppy ear—but not before I had to make another naked bunny for my sister, who was also expecting.

A year or so passed before another cuddly bunny needed to be lovingly sewn, placed in tissue paper, and promptly shipped by Purolator.

No phone call.

Did they get it? What do I do now? I wondered as I waited for Jim to come home from work. Finally, later that evening, we got the awaited response.

"We received the package, and I noticed it was from Jim's work. So I made Dad open it when he arrived home," Mom sheepishly admitted. "Seven? Are you sure you'll be okay?"

I knew she was concerned about my physical and emotional wellbeing, as I would probably be if I were in her shoes. I felt certain she loved each of my kids, but right now, she was just concerned for me. Lovingly, I told her from my heart that God gives us no more than we can handle, and I could do all things with Him.

My one and only brother, James, got married a short time later. My sister and I had our children go up on stage at the evening wedding reception, each with their own bunnies. My oldest daughter, Desiree, encouraged the unsuspecting couple to the front. She presented her Uncle James and new Aunt Jane with a special gift—a naked bunny. She quickly related to everyone how the bunnies came to be, then explained that this gift was not one they were allowed to keep. Instead, this gift was a way for them to tell Opa and Oma Van Tuyl that the next generation of Van Tuyls would finally arrive. Later we heard that this bunny travelled to Holland with Mom, Dad, James, and Jane. While in Holland, at a house they borrowed, the bunny showed up at breakfast one morning, silently telling their exciting news.

Knowing my mom would probably not open another Purolator package, I tried a different approach. My sister Monica had just had another baby boy, and his bunny sat naked at my mom's house. So I placed a set of boy clothes in a box for Jim to ship to my mom (and dad). On top of the set of clothes, I had attached a note that read: "Bet you thought this was another bunny?" Again, Dad had to open the precious package, as Mom would have nothing to do with it (as if she could stop the inevitable).

"It's only a set of bunny clothes for Kurtis' bunny," he informed her.

"Dig deeper," Mom instructed. She knew me well, for there was another naked bunny in the bottom of the box with a note of its own. It read, "Yep, you were right!"

Shortly after the box was shipped came the shocking news! My brother and his wife, Jane, were expecting triplets!

"Monica, we don't have to have a baby this year!" I joked. "Jane is going to have one for each of us!"

She laughed, but two weeks later, she called and sheepishly informed me that I had to sew a fourth naked bunny.

One evening from behind my sewing machine, I stated, "Jim, I'm really starting to hate bunnies."

"I don't know why you made rabbits. You know how they multiply," came the witty reply.

I can't remember all the bunny delivery stories, but another one sticks out. For this "announcement," we visited my parents for a combined Mother's Day and Father's Day. We gift-bagged the naked bunny for Dad and another long-forgotten gift for Mom. Then, as instructed, the kids ran ahead of us into the house, through the usual basement door, and up the stairs to the living room. Half of them circled Opa, and the other half circled Oma. I hid in the stairwell, carefully watching my father's face. Dad peeked into his gift bag and smiled. He looked up to see me half-hidden in the stairway, winked at me, and made an announcement.

"I think I have the wrong gift, Oma! I think this one is for you."

Mom, surrounded by grandkids, excitedly admired her gift. "No, I don't think so," she responded, looking up at Dad. "Why? What did you get?"

Dad handed her his gift bag. Then, curiously, she removed the tissue paper. Immediately her eyes widened and her head shot up, searching the room for me. I sheepishly came up the rest of the stairs and showed off my already-growing belly. It took her a minute or two for the news to register, then, in spite of it all, she congratulated me with a genuine smile and a huge hug.

One day after this, we noticed the space in front of my parents' fireplace became a little roomier as the bunnies were finally moved to the rec room downstairs. So this is where those nineteen fluffy bunnies, thirteen overall-clad and six dress and bloomer-clad, now take residence, or so I thought!

One cold, snowy day in January, about six years later, my oldest daughter, Desiree, was married. At her evening wedding reception, my smiling mother and father carried a big box to the front. After taking the microphone, my mom called up my equally pleased younger niece and nephews. They all took a minute surrounding the box. Then, when they turned around, they each held a few fully clothed bunnies in their arms.

"Well, Desiree," my mom began, "as you know, your mom made bunnies for me whenever she or your aunts were expecting another grandchild for us. But somewhere along the line, she made an extra bunny. So instead of the nineteen bunnies, she actually made twenty. Is there something you wanted us to know, Joanne?" she questioned me as everyone turned to look at me expectantly.

"*No!*" I laughed. "I was wondering if I made an extra one, but I lost count."

"Well, Desiree and Joseph, today we give you this extra naked bunny for when you have to tell your parents the good news of their first grandchild." Mom passed the extra naked bunny to Desiree and added, "Desiree, now you will have to take over the job of making naked bunnies for your family. I think if you each have ten children as your parents did, you only have to make one hundred bunnies!"

The day of our twenty-fifth anniversary appeared, and so did Desiree and Joseph's naked bunny! I made Desiree take it back. No matter how cute and cuddly they were, I didn't want to see another fluffy flannel bunny again. My daughters, wanting to keep with tradition, were now talking about starting me in a mini-scale bunny figurine collection, since flannel bunnies are out of the question. Maybe I can handle this new adventure, but they better remember … bunnies tend to multiply!

You know you have a large family when ...
- The dentist runs out of different styles of toothbrushes for everyone in your large family to have a different one.
- You cancel a dentist appointment due to illness, and the hygienists get the afternoon off.
- You can rearrange the kids' dental appointments so that you can be in at the same time as the youngest, so no one has to babysit the younger ones while you get your teeth cleaned.
- You turn from the reception desk at the dentist's office to see four lovely hygienists lined up at attention, waiting to take your children to get their teeth cleaned.

"I have Calvin. Can we take X-rays, and are there any medical changes?" questions the first.

"This is Calvin," I say, pointing to the child. "Yes, you may do X-rays, and there are no medical changes. Next!" I jokingly say with a smile.

"I have Joshua," says the next hygienist, looking in her file with a smile. Actually, they are all smiling now, playing this game with me as we go through the first bunch of kids.!

Seventeen
Inconvenience

*"And surely I am with you always,
to the very end of the age"*
(Matthew 28:20b).

INCONVENIENCE. I'VE BEEN thinking a lot about this word lately, so much so that I looked it up in *The World Book Dictionary*.[3]

Inconvenience: 1. lack of convenience or ease; trouble; bother SYN: discomfort, disadvantage, incommodity. 2. something inconvenient; cause of trouble, difficulty, or bother.

A mother knows inconvenience. She knows discomfort. She knows difficulty. For example, while teaching a child a difficult lesson, another wants a drink and/or snack. Maybe you're reading a good book, and the smell coming from the toddler is redirecting your thoughts. Someone is calling (or yelling) your name from the other side of the house while you're in the middle of making dinner, potatoes boiling, hands deep in the ground beef. The dishes are piling up, and your distraught teenager walks by quietly, looking at the dirty floor. You know something is up; you have to leave those

---

[3] Clarence Lewis Barnhart, *The World Book Dictionary,* s.v. "inconvenience" (Marshall Field, ILL: Field Enterprises Educational Corp, 1977).

dishes and show that child that they're more important. Later at night, you climb longingly into your bed when a chatty teenager dives in on the other side (or between you and your husband), ready to talk!

A mom needs to welcome inconvenience, especially in a large family. This is how she shows those around her that they are loved. We must be willing to drop all that "stuff" happening around us at the drop of a hat to be inconvenienced. Are you willing to do that? Your willingness to *stop*, sit, and listen is what they want—I dare say, what they need.

Our children need to know we are there for them. We need to show them Christ. Is He not always there for us? Is He not always there to listen and to hold our hand? He even tells us that things in this world won't be easy, but we need to go through them. Paul reassures us of this in Romans 5:3–5:

> Not only so, but we also glory in our sufferings, because we know that suffering produces perseverance; perseverance, character; and character, hope. And hope does not put us to shame, because God's love has been poured out into our hearts by the Holy Spirit, who has been given to us.

But during these challenging times, we can be reassured that He will be there beside us: "*And surely I am with you always, to the very end of the age*" (Matthew 28:20b). Your life is not falling apart. It is falling into place! How well are you willing to be inconvenienced?

Family at Large

You know you have a large family when ...

- You want to help your daughter after she has your first grandbaby, only to have to find a babysitter for your own kids.
- You go to the hospital to meet your new grandchild, and your husband asks the nurses if the siblings can come in. They say yes, and six kids ranging in age from eighteen down to six walk down the hall. The nurses' mouths slowly drop open, and their eyes grow wide. "Are they all from the same house?" "Yes," my husband states while quickly directing them down the hall to where our daughter, the new mom, is waving an encouraging hand. Soon we are told to leave. "Unless you guys live in a commune or something, you must leave." Thankfully, our daughter texted us a short time later, saying that they were leaving the hospital and we were to meet them at their house.

Eighteen
A Large Family Sort of Day

THE DAY BEGAN as usual, preparing Jim's lunch for work, but it wouldn't be for long. Within a few minutes, we turned to a little voice saying, "I have to go pee!"

Two of our grandchildren had spent the night while their parents, our son Nico and his wife, Jodi, spent two days concentrating on moving to a new house. Then, within another fifteen minutes, our son Derek came in the door with his two little ones, ready for a fun day at Grandma's because daycare was closed today. Now with a smile on his face, Jim, known as Papa, was trying to get ready for work while answering many little people's questions. A time he always treasured!

As Jim left for work, I entertained the little ones while the rest of the house slowly stirred. Joshua, still entertaining a significantly bad sunburn, slowly entered. He was followed by Calvin a bit later, complaining about all the little people's mess. Rubbing her eyes, Victoria checked the time to see if she could fit in her daily workout. Groggily, Melissa was ready to hit the books to get ahead in school with her summer English course before going to the barn to care for a horse.

At 9:00, after a night shift at work, Elly entered into a bombardment of questions:

"Are we going to make a cake today, Aunt Elly?"

"Can we do a craft, Aunt Elly?"

Partway through the morning, I got a phone call. Jodi wanted to know if we could dog-sit Ella, as she was getting underfoot. Ella was one of those purse dogs. The kids loved her, and she loved the kids. But the trick was to sneak Ella in without the kids seeing Mom and Dad. So Ella mysteriously arrived mid-morning, while Victoria mysteriously disappeared to help with the move.

Papa Facetimed at lunch. It made his day: "I love you, Papa! We miss you, Papa!" amidst all the other thousand questions.

Meanwhile, by late morning, Elly (after a hair and nails party with the two little girls) joined Melissa and took the little girls to the horse barn to see the animals. An adventure all its own! After lunch, we switched up the naps as the phone rang. It was Nathan, wondering if Calvin could come to help with yard work at his place. A little bit later, the phone rang again. Christina was doing Scentsy deliveries with her friend, and the three kids (her eleven-month-old and her friend's thirteen-month-old twins) needed a break.

"Can we come and let the kids get out for a bit?"

"Sure, the more the merrier."

So as the kids arrived, Nathan drove out with Calvin and an extra push mower. As we entered the house, Elly was busy preparing a meal for her oldest sister, Desiree, for when she went there tomorrow. Christina and her friend didn't stay long and were soon on their way again. Danielle, Derek's wife, entered to pick up their two kids. She was off to Nico and Jodi's new house to help.

"Just leave the kids here to play. They haven't finished baking the cake with Aunt Elly yet, and I had promised a swim in the kiddy pool."

So off she went.

A Large Family Sort of Day

After a swim party, cake decorating, and supper with cake for dessert, Nico and Jodi came to drop off Victoria and pick up their kids. Derek snuck in there somewhere to get his two munchkins. The house was a buzz. After everyone left, Elly worked on the dishes while Victoria cleaned up the toys. As we were nearly done, Calvin entered from a hot afternoon with his brother. By the time Papa returned home, the house was too quiet.

"Where are all my little people?" he asked sadly.

With a big sigh, I sit and wonder what tomorrow will bring. You never know.

You know you have a large family when ...
- *People assume you know every other large family in a two-hour radius.*
- *You move into a new-to-you house in a small town, and everyone knows you're coming.*

Nineteen
Things People Say!

COUNTLESS TIMES I run errands in town with only five or six of my (hopefully) delightful children. Thinking I am probably babysitting, curious people ask if they are all my children.

I love to reply, "No, the rest are at home," and watch the look on their faces as the statement sinks in. Guaranteed, a shocked look will come with, "How many children *do* you have?"

My friend Christine and I attended a lovely bridal shower for our dear friend Pam. The three of us, friends from high school, had stayed close over the years. This shower took place during those tough years when I didn't attend many functions alone, always having a nursing child with me. Well, this particular night I had my baby daughter Victoria with me, and like at most places, people wanted to hold my baby girl. It was only a short time before the talkative lady beside me politely asked if she too could hold Victoria.

"Sure," I responded, handing Victoria over to her.

Unfortunately, not long after Victoria got into her eager hands, she began to fuss. Feeling sorry for the lady, I suggested she lay Victoria across her lap and pat her back.

"She likes that," I encouraged.

The lady sympathetically looked at me and asked, "Is this your first?" I heard Christine beside me stifling a giggle.

"This is my fifth," I quietly answered.

"Your *fifth*?" she blurted out.

Then, not believing me, she looked at the bride, Pam, asking her to verify that this was indeed my fifth child.

Pam's face lit up with a smile, and she confidently affirmed, "Yes!"

"But you two are the same age. You went to high school together, right?"

We both nodded our heads. She struggled to grasp our answer and kept repeating, "I just can't believe it—five kids!"

We have a son who, in high school, didn't want many people to know he came from a large family. While in grade nine at the local Catholic high school, it seemed to be his biggest kept secret. Not hanging out much with his older brother in grade eleven certainly helped to keep his secret. Then, two years later, his younger sister arrived in grade nine.

"Are you related to Nathan?" they would ask her.

"Yes, he's my brother," she would politely answer.

"Oh, I didn't know he had a sister," they'd respond with slight surprise. But knowing her brother didn't want everyone to know, she did what any real sister would.

"Actually, he has five sisters," she would state as one side of her mouth curled into a smile. Then, as the shock grew on their faces, she'd continue, "and four brothers!" The full, sisterly grin appeared while the questioner tried to pick their jaw off the ground.

Family at Large

As a fun-loving salesman for a used tractor and heavy equipment yard, Jim talked to many thrifty farmers trying to get an exceptional deal. One persistent customer didn't like Jim's initial price and wanted it lowered considerably.

"How am I supposed to put shoes on my kids' feet for that price?" Jim jokingly replied.

Thinking he had Jim beat, the customer said, "Well, I think my kids need shoes more!"

Up for the challenge, Jim replied, "Whoever has more kids gets the price they're asking."

"Deal," the customer confidently declared! "Beat six kids!"

Trying not to gloat, Jim replied with a smile, "I have ten!"

"Who do I make the cheque out to?" came the defeated reply.

Another day as Jim was working, a customer started talking about life with his five girls.

"I have five girls too. It's great!" Jim replied.

A short time later in the conversation, the happy farmer, thinking he had found someone who understood, jokingly commented about not knowing how to make boys. To which Jim honestly confessed he also had five boys.

Shocked, the farmer responded curiously, "How do you do that?"

Smiling, Jim responded, "You put your hat on backward."

I was asked to speak on home organization for my mom's church's Coffee Break group. This wonderful group of multi-aged ladies were eager to listen, especially when they heard I had ten kids.

"She must know what she's talking about."

"She must be a Super Mom!"

Honestly, I wouldn't say I like the term Super Mom, so I discussed this with my mom afterward.

"Mom, I am no Super Mom. I don't know how to get that across to people clearly. I'm just a regular mom like them who happens to have a few more kids. There are countless days in which I don't feel I can do it. I know I can only do it with the Lord's help. Having as many kids as I do sure makes me rely more on Him. Do you think the moms with two or three kids depend on Him? Is that as many kids as *they* can handle? Maybe they'd learn to trust God more if they left their comfort zone of what *they* think they could handle." My thoughts slowly tumbled out as I pondered Philippians 4:13: *"I can do all this through him who gives me strength."*

My mind travelled back to a memorable yet challenging summer after the birth of my sixth child. This particular summer, I was at my wits' end and felt I could no longer do this mom thing. I wanted out! Instead, God sent an incredible friend to me. Every week as we sat in our back yards watching our happy kids play, we talked, laughed, and cried together about what was happening in our daily lives. We looked up relevant verses weekly, sharing God's promises for us. That summer, I realized an awesome God was in control of my out-of-control life. I could do nothing without Him. From then on, I daily looked to Him for love and comfort. When things happen now, I can still feel myself being sucked into the "I can't do it!" feeling, but then I remember that He is there and promises to take care of everything.

Mom had listened intently, thinking as my mind had travelled back in time. Then, breaking into my thoughts, she responded, "Maybe you just need to tell them what you just told me. It isn't that you're a Super Mom, but you have a Super God!"

Family at Large

You know you have a large family when ...

- *Your oldest daughter pleads to have her own room. The best you can do is give her one with her new baby sister. After only two weeks, she returns to you, wanting to move back in with her three sisters. When you ask why, she answers, "I miss reading to my sisters at night." So it's not long before you take the wall out between the two rooms for the five sisters to share, with two sets of bunk beds and a crib.*
- *Your first grandchild has a wardrobe full of "Best Uncle" and "Awesome Aunt" t-shirts.*
- *Your daughter changes your grandson's diaper in one bathroom, and your youngest son calls you to help him from another.*

Twenty
Thoughts from My Parenting Experience
By Jim Schreuders (Oct. 2012)

RAISING OUR CHILDREN is an incredible journey filled with continual insights and lessons on humility. This fact brings me back to when I was trying to teach my oldest to ride his bicycle. He didn't learn anything when I held on too tightly to the seat. When in frustration I completely let him go, and he rolled down the barn hill until he crashed into the shed, he became angry and discouraged. Yet as long as I ran alongside him, encouraging him and occasionally steadying him, he continued to improve and gain confidence.

I could have learned a lot from that experience had I been paying attention. Instead, in my pride and ignorance, I was too focused on the goal of being the teacher rather than looking for a life lesson of my own.

The challenges continued into grade school, adolescent, and teen years. It took me that long to let go of my pride, open my eyes, and let my children teach me more than a few things. I can't deny that I still have great dreams for my children, but I can at least now humbly accept that they are their own distinct and unique persons with their own goals, being created by God for His own purpose (Not ours!). I now move alongside them gently and in love, correcting them, showing grace and forgiveness on a constant basis, as Paul says in Colossians 3:13b, *"Forgive as the Lord forgave you."*

So how does this play out? First, I've learned never to react out of anger but to focus on a loving approach in all circumstances. That takes loads of self-control, but I use my lifeline of prayer to my Heavenly Father to help with that. Anger will never result in a positive reaction but in separation and bitterness, whereas love will always leave the door open for reconciliation.

Second, I show respect to my children, acknowledging even their most ridiculous ideas, and offering in a loving way my own wisdom and ideas.

Third, I let them make their mistakes and continue loving and respecting them even if I'm extremely disappointed. This is probably one of the most difficult things to do, but I always think about the prodigal son and how he was still able to come home despite his foolishness. First Peter 4:8 says, *"Above all, love each other deeply, because love covers over a multitude of sins."*

We are vessels of love to our children and need God's love to shine through us. These children are not really ours but God's. We need to allow God's will to work out in these precious children, which is something we can thankfully count on in faith. This means that despite our great plans, our children's lives are really not in our control. But as we run along beside them less and less, we eventually will let them go, knowing that God will be with them.

This is an ongoing process in which the final chapter will be written in eternity. The difficult challenges will continue until then. In the meanwhile, there is still plenty to learn. The older I get, it seems the more I realize just how little I really know. So we simply carry on in the strength God gives us from day to day, continually seeking His wisdom.

Proverbs 9:10: *"The fear of the Lord is the beginning of wisdom, and knowledge of the Holy One is understanding."*

Also by Joanne Schreuders

Doing It Well

WALKING THROUGH CANCER WITH HOPE

Joanne Schreuders

ISBN: 978-1-4866-2548-2

Do you, or does someone you know, have cancer? Do you want to know how you can help make this rollercoaster ride a little easier? Jim did it well. Leaning on God, Jim strived to keep humour and normalcy in everyday life. He walked through the things he was losing with his family, preparing them for the future. Are you doing it well?